BODÉ ABODERIN

FATHERHOOD BY PAPA B

A GAME-CHANGING GUIDE FOR PARENTS, FATHER FIGURES, AND FATHERS TO BE

TO MY CHILDREN

RENAE, ESMÉ-OLIVIA & RICHARD-JUNIOR

CONTENTS

FATHERHOOD IS LIT

I'm meant to start this book by telling you who I am, but that's a really open question. What does that mean? I feel like I'm in therapy – and as much as you'll find out that I am a fan of therapy, it's also not my first instinct to bare all so easily. But I'm Bodé. I'm a father of three – Renae who's thirteen, Esmé who's eight, and RJ who's three – and husband to Candice, business owner. I'm well into cars, I like to play a bit of golf in my spare time, and I dabble in a bit of venture capitalism. I'm a boring geezer really, but this actually works in my favour when it comes to this book because, well, I'm like everyone else.

My life experiences may differ slightly from yours in the details, but I think you'll find they're relatable. Hopefully that makes the different stages I've gone through – deconstructing and reconstructing myself and my ideas about fatherhood, family, and masculinity – accessible to you too.

When I moved to the UK from Nigeria in 2003 for university, it was an absolute culture shock. I saw things I'd always longed for growing up in Nigeria, but did not know how to express at the time. I saw a balanced family set-up that I wished was practised back home. Accepting this was difficult at first, I must admit, but that is what this book is about: it is about my journey from boyhood to manhood and then fatherhood. How I transitioned from one to the next, and how I realised that what I felt back then – the unease that came from my dad's expectations versus my desire to live differently – was real and valid.

In all honesty, I'm not coming here to preach, expecting you to listen and follow everything I say or have done. I'm just hoping you'll relate. I believe we've all got things to share with the world, no matter how boring we may be, so maybe there's something you can learn from me and my mistakes.

I wanted to write this book to dispel myths. There are loads of myths and beliefs that, in the grand scheme of things, when you deconstruct them, are a load of crap. There is all this stuff that was constructed to protect the male ego, further promote the patriarchy, and protect the status quo as a whole.

My goal is for people – for men most especially – to read this book and start to question their beliefs, or what they've been taught to believe. I want you to look closely at these ideas and question them. I'm not expecting you to finish this book and be completely changed or be more like me, but I just want to get you thinking, to get your thought process started, to look at things another way.

Because things can always change for the better.

So now I'm going to ask you a question.

Who are you?

What do you believe about fatherhood and masculinity, and why do you believe it? Think deeply about this. A lot of the time, when we really begin to think on these things, many of us realise that something's not working how we'd like it to.

This is my journey. This is what I realised. This is what wasn't working for me. And this is how I changed it.

I want this book to be thought-provoking, sure. I want it to encourage you to think about parenting in a different way. But I also want it to be helpful. It's not just about the ideas but about the steps – big and small – you can take to make real changes to your mindset, and to your life. Each chapter ends with some practical ideas – quick tips, questions to ask yourself, or ideas of things you can do with your kids – that I hope will help you feel confident to start making a change.

Take from it what you will, but – spoiler alert – I will unapologetically tell you that the concept of the alpha male and all the toxic masculinity associated with it helps no one – not you, your partner, your children, your family, or society as a whole. Don't believe me? Don't worry, we'll get into it later, but first, a bit more about me and where I come from...

LOOK AT THINGS ANOTHER WAY

CHAPTER 1

ORIGINS

"Those who forget their past are destined to repeat it."

— Robert A Heinlein

I was born and raised for half of my life in Lagos, Nigeria. Lagos is the largest city and former capital of Nigeria and the largest megacity on the African continent in terms of population (estimated at 14.3 million people).

Lagos is a city where people come from neighbouring towns and villages to chase a dream, to find work, to make something of themselves, and to provide the means to build something back home – 'home' meaning whatever town or state they are originally from. In my case, I trace my roots back to Ibadan, the most populous city in Oyo State, about a two-and-a-half-hour drive from Lagos.

Ibadan is a city with a rich history. It was originally a military base for Yoruba warriors in the 1800s but grew into a bustling trade centre and an important transit point within Nigeria. It is home to many firsts: the first TV station in the whole of Africa opened there in 1959 and Nigeria's oldest surviving newspaper, the *Nigerian Tribune*, is also published there. Nigeria's first skyscraper – Cocoa House – is located there, as is Nigeria's first university, now known as the University of Ibadan.

My father has always been quite proud of where our family is from. The Aboderin name is a pretty well-known name in Ibadan, in Nigeria and beyond, and this is largely due to the success of many of the family's sons and daughters, and also quite a few historical events that I didn't care enough to know as a youngster.

One of the historical events to note began with a late, well-known first cousin once removed of mine, Chief James Olubunmi Aboderin. He studied history in the mid-fifties at North Western Polytechnic in the UK, a precursor to London Metropolitan University. While in the city, he took the Institute of Chartered Accountants exam and was admitted in May 1964. He later went on to start one of the most successful newspaper houses in Nigeria, the widely read *Punch* newspaper, which still remains in circulation today. Olu Aboderin was instrumental in my father's upbringing. He was Dad's older cousin, and he even paid for Dad's education in the UK, where he studied from 1977–1980. Afterwards, Dad returned to Nigeria to take on the job of marketing and advertising manager at *Punch*. My mother was the newspaper's librarian and they met and got married in 1981, and I was born four years later.

The Aboderin family is what some might class as 'elite'. The English translation of the Aboderin name is 'we walk with the hunters', and our family has always had an entrepreneurial spirit that is present to this day. Your family name can take you really far in Nigeria, and sometimes further in the world, and I have lost count of how many times the mention of my name has opened doors for me. I don't share this to boast, but to explain why, as a child, there was a huge focus on how

I behaved outside of the home and I always felt a heavy weight in terms of trying not to bring shame to the family name. I still remember Dad saying over and over, 'Remember the son of whom you are!'

Nigerian culture was and still is patriarchal, and this explains why there is a void in my knowledge of Mum's family. As a woman, once you get married into a family, you become part of that family, and it is almost as if everything that made you who you are ceases to exist. Personally, I find that hard to accept. Why is it acceptable to erase a woman's history? There is a lot of literature about the word 'history' but not about 'herstory'.

What I do know is that Mum came from another Yoruba family that hailed from another south-western state called Ogun State. Ogun State has its own history, of course, and is well known for the town Abeokuta, which houses the popular tourist attraction, Olumo Rock. Olumo Rock is a massive outcrop of granite rocks and Abeokuta translates as 'under a rock' in English. The rock is a historical monument, important because it served as a shelter and fortress for the Egba people during the intercity wars between rival Yoruba clans. This is just how I see my role as a father: my job is to provide shelter and protection to my children. I am constantly working to ensure they feel safe and secure regardless of where they find themselves.

Growing up, I could see that my mum and dad were very different and I often wondered as a child how they got together. Mum is quite reserved, shy, and quiet, very artistic and quite the writer and strategist – and an absolute beauty! Dad, on the other hand, can be the loudest in the room, quite overpowering and oftentimes he steals the show. He is not shy or quiet, not strategic at all, but he knows how to command the attention of a lot of people. You will spot my dad from a mile off. All this meant that you probably never saw or heard from the woman of the house – my mother – the matriarch, the glue, the person who held it all together, and quite frankly, the one who had the most influence on my values as they are today.

Three years after I was born, my twin sisters, Bade and Yode, came along. So I grew up in a family of five. We lived in a four-bedroom house on a private estate. The house was perfect for us. We had a huge back garden where Dad kept all his livestock: goats, rabbits, turkeys, chickens, and large African snails. We had a garage big enough to fit three cars in it, as well as a big drive and a large, steel security gate. I had a big room to myself, which had a double bed as well as a bunk bed for when cousins or friends came over. The living area was open plan and contained a lot of bookshelves, large sofas, and a TV across from the front door. On the other side of the room was the family dining table, which was large enough to seat ten people.

Growing up in Lagos was great. There was a wonderful sense of community, so you were never really brought up by your parents alone. Because of this, you had to make sure you were never caught taking part in any activity deemed as below the standards set by your family because, rest assured, details of said activity would reach your home before you did! Mrs Agboola or some other auntie or uncle would see you and decide to run straight to your parents to inform them. They would also wait at your home to take part in what

YOU WILL SPOT MY DAD FROM A MILE OFF. ALL THIS MEANT THAT YOU PROBABLY NEVER SAW OR HEARD FROM THE WOMAN OF THE HOUSE – MY MOTHER – THE MATRIARCH, THE GLUE, THE PERSON WHO HELD IT ALL TOGETHER.

some might call a 'family meeting', though it was really more of a public takedown.

To an extent, I have tried to raise my children with this same sense of community by establishing a group of trusted people around us who are ready to step in, in my absence.

Lagos is the place where I learned to drive – without my dad's permission or knowledge. One day, I took one of his cars out on a joyride whilst he and my mum were at work. The joyride in itself was successful; I was able to show off to my friends that I was now a big boy – I was whipping! However, it all came crashing down when I took out the gate to the family compound as I tried to park the car exactly the way I'd found it.

Funnily enough, this was one time I felt I was going to get the biggest licks of my life, since Dad was a fan of corporal punishment – but surprisingly this did not happen. Dad took one look at me, said nothing, and enrolled me in driving lessons the very next day. But I did have to wash all our cars for the next month or two.

I had my early education in Lagos and I went to a few schools that would be classed as 'independent' or private and exclusive here in the UK. The secondary school I attended was called King's College, Lagos – yes, you read that right. King's College was set up by, you guessed it, the British in 1909. The school admits only male students, although historically, some female HSC (A-level equivalent) students were admitted before the establishment of Queen's College, Lagos – King's College's sister school, which my sisters attended.

Let's just say I had a very British secondary school education. The philosophy of King's College was,

'To provide for the youth of the Colony a higher general education than that supplied by the existing schools, to prepare them for the Matriculation Examination of the University of London, and to give a useful course of study to those who intend to qualify for professional life or to enter Government or Mercantile service.'[1] Basically, the aim of the school was to train the children of the Nigerian elite in the British way, extending the colonial influence of Britain.

Our school uniform consisted of a white shirt (long-sleeved for those in the senior school and short-sleeved for those in the junior school), a school tie and/or a school badge, white trousers, black belt, black socks, black laced shoes, and a blue blazer. I took part in sports that included cricket, polo, squash, and athletics – which I was particularly good at. My school house was called Hyde Johnson, named after one of the school's principals from 1910. King's College Old Boys (what former students of the school are known as) have a bond, a very strong one, and will often acknowledge their school days with shouts of the word '*Floreat!*' which is Latin for 'flourish' and the first word of the school anthem.

As well as the influence of a very British secondary school education, we were brought up with traditional Yoruba values, such as the need to prostrate, which is the act of lying stretched out on the ground with one's face downwards anytime you met with someone who was older than you, and the importance of being quiet when adults are talking. Yoruba culture as a whole is very deferential to elders by default, and as a child your views did not matter and you basically had to do as you were told even if you were not comfortable with it.

I HAVE SUCCESSFULLY EXTRACTED THE PARTS OF THAT CULTURE I FEEL COMFORTABLE WITH AND DISCARDED ANYTHING THAT BLOCKS THE DEVELOPMENT OF MY CHILDREN IN TERMS OF THEIR ABILITY TO EXPRESS THEMSELVES.

The Yoruba values are values I struggle with at times. I have successfully extracted the parts of that culture I feel comfortable with and discarded anything that blocks the development of my children in terms of their ability to express themselves.

The church was also an important part of my upbringing. I distinctly remember the anxiety every Friday, knowing full well that in a few hours we were going to embark on a long, traffic-filled journey to church. Sometimes the journey took three to four hours, only for us to spend two hours in the church listening to the pastor telling you to donate ten per cent of your earnings as tithe to the church in order to receive blessings from God. Believe it or not, I had to pay tithe from my pocket money every month because Dad felt it was good practice. All of this probably explains my current love-hate relationship with the idea of travelling to any place of worship. It is not because I no longer believe in God or that I am no longer spiritual, but it is just that I made a promise to myself back then that once I was an adult and in charge of myself, I would not travel to any church. (My therapist will call this something else and we'll get into this more later.)

Even when I was a child, Dad expected a lot from me. This came with the territory of being a male child in a Nigerian/Yoruba family. Now, throw in the fact that I was the firstborn and the only male child, and it was a lot. There was no room for error – absolutely none – and where my sisters would get a pass, I got a smack. This led to some ill feelings towards my sisters. I saw myself as the 'naughty' one and my sisters as the ones who could do no wrong and, as a result, for a while we had no real relationship. You see, they looked up to me as their big brother, the one they admired, their protector; I saw them as a burden I couldn't wait to run away from.

Over the years, our relationship has become stronger and better and I have learned to love them as my sisters. Although we live in different parts of the world, we are in constant communication and I have come to embody that role of big brother and protector. I wear that badge with honour now, but they had to meet me halfway. They had come to understand why I felt the way I did, so they made an effort to connect with me more. They would often call me just to find out how I was doing, and they wouldn't give up until I opened up to them. They seemed to know exactly what buttons to push and they simply did not accept my excuses. For example, there was a time one of them, Yode to be exact, called just to find out how I was, and I made a move to dismiss her by saying I was busy and I would give her a call later. This was often my go-to excuse but she responded by saying, 'This is what you said last week and two days ago. What is it that you are doing that is more important than telling me how you are? After all, I do care about you and I want to ensure that all is well.'

You see, Bade and Yode are the most lovely set of humans. When we were not as close as we are now, they made the effort to reach out to me. They let me know that they love and care for me, and for this I am eternally grateful.

But back to my parents: Dad had the ethos, 'spare the rod and spoil the child' – a term that will be familiar to anyone who has grown up in a church context. As a result, his approach to our upbringing was very authoritarian and he was distant. Mum was the total opposite – she was warm, kind, and more emotional. She was that shoulder to lean on when needed, though she did not mess about if I ever took the piss.

Growing up, I often found Dad quite draining. You know that presence that makes you freeze and always try to be on your 'A' game? That was him. There was no room for mistakes because making a mistake was not a mistake at all, it was just downright stupidity. I remember a time *I* got smacked because one of my little sisters was running and fell and injured her forehead. Of course, it made no sense to me at the time why I got smacked for that – and I still can't make sense of it. I was a young boy at the time, no older than nine. I was out playing with my friends and we were engaged in a sixty-metre race. According to Dad, I should have been aware of my surroundings to the point that I knew my little sisters were running behind us.

'How on earth was I supposed to do that?' I kept asking myself and my mum later on that day, but somehow it made sense to Dad. In fact, I even asked him about that scenario last year and guess what? He gave me the exact same answer. Let's just say I have buried the chance of getting an answer that makes sense to me. I have come to realise that his way of dealing with things is just what he knows and understands.

My relationship with Mum was different. Often referred to as 'Mama Bodé', *she* was the one to go to when you needed a hug or a pat on the head. She was always there with open arms to give me that much needed warmth. I was always by her side – much to my

WEAR THAT BADGE WITH HONOUR

dad's dislike. 'You do not want to be a woman's wrapper,' he often said. (A wrapper is a length of fabric wrapped around a woman's waist as a skirt in traditional Yoruba dress.) But I did not care; I went where the warmth was. And I know the significance of that for my own children.

A few years after Mum and Dad got married, Mum had to give up work. She continued to run a few businesses here and there, so she was always busy and always entrepreneurial, but she was what we would call a full-time housewife. This is what was expected: the man went out to work and the woman stayed home to look after the children and household. I know she hated it. She continues to mention this fact to this day, but her being a housewife meant I spent a lot of time with her at home and out and about. I was always with her, even when she was visiting with friends, and I still refer fondly to these women as 'Mummy' too. I saw them all as mothers.

Mum believed that a man's place was in the kitchen as much as a woman's and she had me in there all the time, learning how to cook and clean. My dad also hated that; he wanted me sat in the living room watching the news – yes, the fucking news – at seven, eight, nine years old! When I did sit in the living room with him, I used to fall asleep, only to be awoken by a pair of slippers thrown my way.

Dad had a lot of friends, but he thought of his friends in different categories – and those categories never mixed, because this was his way. He had his friends at the auto technicians workshop, who he would sit with to discuss local politics and engage in a game of draughts or Ludo; he had friends at his social clubs for tennis, golf, swimming or business. He held a number of memberships at various country clubs, like Lagos Country Club and Ikoyi Club, and it was here that the elite of Lagos society met. Many business deals were struck in those clubs and this was where you would rub shoulders with the movers and shakers of the country. But Mum had no interest in such things. She has always liked her friendship groups close and tight, and they all had one thing in common: the dislike of the patriarchal set-up of the country. But it was a set-up they could do nothing about.

The way I see it, Dad wanted me to be a man, and a man in his definition was stoic and emotionless, whilst Mum wanted me to be a human. Dad disliked my personality. He saw me as soft, and this was largely because somehow, in his head, he wanted me to someday take over his position as leader, as the head of the family. And not just our immediate family – I'm referring to the wider Aboderin family! I had no interest in that and I still don't. Being a boy child, and the only one at that, you are expected to act accordingly, you are expected to take up that mantle of leadership, you are expected to take your place at the high table while the women take their place in the other room at the back.

This came across in Dad's personality – he was a man who had no space to engage in frivolous things. A man who honestly had no space to feel. I couldn't get with that programme, even as a child. When talking about me, he always threw the word 'defiant' around. He thought I was going out of my way to do the opposite of what he wanted. The truth is, I was just being me – well, I thought I was! Looking back now, and after many a therapy session, I have come to realise that he was just doing what he knew how to do. But still, it didn't change the fact that with my mum it was different; I was allowed to be me. She felt me, she understood me and she provided that much needed balance.

I often get asked who my role model is in terms of fatherhood, and every time I mention the names of people I admire, I am often met with the question: 'But what about your father?' The truth is, I don't mention Dad because what I learned from him was how I *don't* want to be – but more on that later.

FATHERHOOD IN ACTION

When we become parents, caught up in the sleepless nights, nappies, and new routine, a lot of us don't have much opportunity to reflect on our upbringing and the way it shaped our thoughts about family and being a parent. Even in the run-up to becoming a parent, a lot of the time our focus is elsewhere – finding the money we need, getting our home ready, and dealing with all the changes our partners and ourselves are experiencing.

This is a good time to think about the messages you've received through childhood and adolescence about what it means to be a parent. This is something we're going to come back to time and again in the following chapters. You can start by asking yourself the following questions:

What example of family life and parenting did you see from parents, caregivers, and immediate family?

What about your wider community? Was everyone's family set-up similar or different?

As a child, what messages did you absorb about different family set-ups? Was there a 'preferred' way that was presented to you?

What were your thoughts and impressions of this as a child? What do you think about this now?

If you are able to discuss these topics with your own family, it might be interesting to see the different perspectives that your parents, aunties, uncles, siblings, or cousins have. Sometimes their own perceptions of the past can bring up interesting things you haven't yet considered.

CHAPTER 2

MARRIAGE, RELATIONSHIPS & INTIMACY

"We do not develop habits of genuine love automatically. We learn them by watching effective role models — most specifically by observing how our parents express love for each other day in and day out."

– Josh McDowell

Growing up, I had various examples of a union between two people, essentially, what a marriage is. I had my parents and a few close family friends, and very early on I was able to figure out the differences exhibited in their individual set-ups.

My parents, for example, are what a lot of people will class as a 'traditional' family set-up, where the man is the breadwinner, the alpha and omega, the king of the castle. The truth is, whilst I could tell Dad was quite proud of this, I saw how it affected Mum. She was withdrawn and faced each day like a chore. Did I feel that real, hardcore love between them? I am not too sure. You see, these things are pretty difficult to understand.

I will go with my gut feeling though, and that says there was a lack of true happiness in both parties. They had learned to just keep on keeping on – I mean forty or so years of living a certain way will do that to you. Dad expected a full meal when he came home and, no matter the time, he was tended to, looked after, and nurtured. But I often thought to myself, who is nurturing Mum?

I guess I was able to see things this way because I had another couple to compare my parents to. Our next-door neighbours – let's call them the Johnsons – were totally different. They were absolutely equal in their partnership and you could feel the love and respect that flowed through the family. So much so, Dad often made snide comments about Mr Johnson, calling him 'soft'. Then there were the Williamses – they too were different. Mrs Williams was the breadwinner. She was the provider, and it was quite clear how that affected Mr Williams. He was sometimes laughed at by his friends with jokes like, 'We know who wears the trousers in your house!' often thrown around. Even now, you will find Mr Williams trying to assert that the very thing that made him a man was lost the moment his wife started to out-earn him.

I knew without a doubt, back then, which set-up I fancied – it was the Johnsons'. The idea of depending on a woman was a no-no for me – I mean growing up in a family like mine will do that to you. It will make you believe that the moment your significant other starts to out-earn you, you have lost everything; you are no longer able to make decisions. And the worst thing that could ever happen to a man from the society I grew up in is to answer to a woman.

As it happens, while I've been writing this book, now a father to three kids, my family set-up has become one that Dad would have totally frowned upon. I have left full-time employment to create something of my own, which means that, for a certain period of time, my partner, my wife, Candice, will automatically become the breadwinner of our household, while I find my feet.

THE WORST THING THAT
COULD EVER HAPPEN TO
A MAN FROM THE SOCIETY
I GREW UP IN IS TO ANSWER
TO A WOMAN.

But I had a whole lot to learn before I reached this point, and this learning happened during the relationships I went on to have.

I hate to be that guy – you know, the one who acts up with one woman, then fixes up when with another – but in the spirit of honesty, I have to go there. You see, I *was* that guy during my first proper relationship. It was the relationship that gave me my first child, Renae, and my patriarchal beliefs were on full blast. I was my father's son and there was no way on earth any woman was going to tell me what to do. After all, I am a man, therefore I'm the king of the castle. I felt my only duty was to provide financially, but even that became an issue when Renae's mother, Sam, started to earn a lot more than me.

Sam was a fully trained social worker, educated to Masters level, which meant she was able to get a high-paying job from the word go. There was a lot of resentment on my part. At the time, I worked in retail, selling mobiles phones at the now defunct Phones 4u, earning a decent wage but not good enough. In addition to this, I loved to party. I was at every party possible, every weekend and sometimes even during the week. Sam, of course, did not like this because it meant I spent valuable time out of the house living it up and spending every penny I had because – after all – no woman could tell me how to spend my money or time.

Every time she brought this up, it became a full-blown argument because I felt she was trying to tell me what to do as well as how to spend my money and time. It became unhealthy and really toxic. Sam, my baby's mother, was doing all she could to hold it together, which took its toll. I now understand how the situation affected her, both physically and emotionally, and let's just say that relationship did not last.

A year after Renae was born, Sam called it quits. She knew she deserved better, and she definitely did. For me, it was a bitter pill to swallow, and for a whole year I felt hard done by. I felt that she was the one at fault and how dare she kick me to the curb like that? I was bitter to the point that I went into a deep depression. This was the first time I'd faced loss on that scale, and deep down inside I craved a family unit. My parents had stuck to it through thick and thin. My mother was not treated particularly well, but she stayed – so how dare Sam skip out on me?

About two weeks after that break up I lost my job – I had lost it all. I had nowhere to go, no money to afford a roof over my head. I was living in a room in Sam's mother's house, receiving £20 a week from my mother's friend. It was the definition of rock bottom and I blamed it all on Sam. I blamed her for all my misfortune. I still did not get it – I even said things like, 'Well, if you didn't leave me, I wouldn't have lost my job!'

My moment of clarity came later, and it started the day I decided to answer Dad's call. He had tried to call me several times before that and I had avoided him – in fact, I avoided everyone. But Dad wanted me to come home to Nigeria for a week or so to refocus and recharge. I agreed and to this day I am unable to explain the relief I felt once the aircraft took off.

Upon arrival in Nigeria, I felt peace on a level I still cannot explain. I mostly spent time with family, and visited my grandmother, whom I shared a strong bond with. Maybe this is because she was, at one point, my mother; she took care of me when my mum was pregnant with my sisters and for a long time after they were born. When I was born, it was my grandmother who gave me my first bath and a whole lot more. She always prayed for me as well. I remain grateful for the time spent with her when I went back to Nigeria as it was the last time I saw her in person. She died of old age a few years later.

Of course, while I was in Nigeria I went to church. I come from a very spiritual family who believe prayer is the best answer in any situation, and you know what, I do too — alongside doing the necessary work. For me, returning to church at that moment provided the family and community vibe that was missing in my life, and once again I felt part of something. Something familiar, something I knew.

Returning to Nigeria as an adult was different in so many ways. Even though I was back at my parents' house only for a short while, there was a certain level of respect I received as an adult that I never got as a child. I wasn't being told what to do. Instead, I was getting advice and a shoulder to lean on. One of the biggest things I noticed was the fact that my parents were working together, and for me this was a bit strange, but in a good way.

You see, in the past, my parents often came from opposing sides when a challenging situation arose. Dad's answer to pretty much everything lacked softness, to say the least. Whereas Mum always used the softer approach, which Dad hated. But when I returned to Nigeria after the breakdown of my relationship and the loss of my job, here were my parents acting like two peas in a pod, singing off the same hymn sheet as if they were one person. Dad was agreeing Mum and vice versa. Looking back on this now, I think it was really important for me to see and experience this. It showed me the power and beauty of an amazing partnership.

One of the best parts of my return was the time I got to spend with Mum. She used our time together to remind me of all she had taught me, and even though she didn't say it outright, she definitely hinted that she thought I was behaving and acting like Dad. She would drop subtle hints by saying things like, 'I remember when your dad did that...' I got the message every time. Thanks, Mum!

One week in Nigeria was enough for me to realise I needed to work on myself and deal with my demons – demons I now realised I had thanks to my trip, to Nigeria, which had given me the time and space to realise I was walking the same path as Dad. I was doing exactly what I'd promised I wouldn't do: I was treating another woman the way Dad treated Mum.

So many years have passed since then and time has given me the chance to really go over the series of events that shaped my actions, to address my behaviour, and face it head on.

I have come to realise that childhood trauma has a way of reappearing in your life later on without you even knowing it's happening. Unprocessed, unresolved, or undealt with childhood trauma is guaranteed to resurface in life at a later stage, and the transition to parenthood can be one of a few major triggers where we can find ourselves struggling.

I STARTED TO DEVELOP MYSELF SPIRITUALLY

David Shemmings, professor of social work at the University of Kent and a specialist in attachment theories, says, '"Unresolved" here has a very precise meaning. For example, it doesn't mean that the person cries at the thought of their loss. The term indicates post-traumatic stress disorder and/or dissociation.'[2]

A lot of us have experienced traumatic episodes and never had an outlet to really deal with them. We may think we're fine as we avoid situations that remind us of that particular trauma, or as we drown out traumatic memories with work, life, and other distractions. But when we are in stressful situations, we may find ourselves replicating the behaviour that we witnessed and swore we'd never do. It's because we haven't addressed these traumas – and deep down, that's all we know.

Growing up, I didn't have a voice or much confidence because Dad was so overwhelming. I often found that any time I was challenged about anything, I hit back with aggression like a livewire because I felt my safe space was being threatened. Fast forward to my relationship with Sam and, whenever she challenged me on my spending or how I spent my time, I reacted in much the same way. As soon as I felt threatened, including when I experienced the loss of my relationship and job, I reverted to the bullshit patriarchal script that I had grown up with.

At the time, I did not understand why Dad called me back to Nigeria or why I listened to him, but one thing I do know is that my time in Nigeria bridged a gap in our relationship. A few years later, I actually asked Dad why he made that call. He said he had spoken to a spiritual leader who told him he had got things pretty wrong in the past, and it was affecting me now. He was advised to make amends and bridge the gap because I needed him.

Maybe a spiritual intervention is exactly what we both needed because for the first time in forever, my dad was there to listen to me talk about how I was feeling without any judgement or lecturing me to be 'strong'. In fact, this was the first time he admitted to getting things wrong. I remember one of our conversations clearly. We were sitting in one of the living rooms in our family home. It felt strange when he asked me the question – perhaps it was a question I had waited all my life to hear from him and better late than never, right? He started by saying, 'I am not really concerned about the why, what I really need to know is how you are feeling and what are your plans?'

This really shocked me and for a second or two I was speechless. But what happened next was really astonishing: we connected in a way we never had before. I actually told him exactly how I was feeling. I told him how I felt all hope was lost and a whole lot more. His response surprised me further; he offered words of encouragement and even told me he had been there before. He told me about the 'Israelites' journey' he'd had to take to achieve anything in life. This was in reference to the Biblical story of the Israelites who, after they escaped from Egypt, were said to have wandered in the wilderness for forty years before finally making it to the Promised Land. Dad explained that he always felt he could have been greater, or done better in his life, if he hadn't made so many mistakes whilst growing up – which meant it took him twice the time to achieve anything. He told me how he hoped the same thing wouldn't happen to me.

He gave me a bit of insight into his childhood, through to adulthood, and how he met Mum. Then he told me he was here for me, that he had my back, and that he was willing to help in any way possible. The first thing he felt I had to do was get a place of my own because he didn't think it was a good idea to go back to staying at Sam's mother's house. In fact, he made a few phone calls there and then to some of his friends with properties for rent in the UK, and once he found something he felt was suitable, he made arrangements for payment himself.

This was truly something. For the first time, I saw Dad really being a dad. In one of my darkest moments, he had connected with me in a way I had longed for all my life.

This encounter really made me think about my feelings, and I began to wish he had always been like that with me. It highlighted the importance of the relationship between father and child, and it made me realise that my acting up was tied to my yearning for a relationship with him. I came to a conclusion: I would ensure that I created this kind of bond with Renae. And if I would go on to have more kids, I needed to ensure that they knew I was there, available for a conversation about their feelings any time, and that I would do my utmost to ensure that door would always remain open.

This was the beginning of my centring; this was the beginning of my rebranding. I had finally realised that I had gotten things absolutely wrong. Most importantly, I needed to strengthen my relationship with Renae's mum, Sam. There was an innocent child in the middle

FOR THE FIRST TIME, I SAW DAD REALLY BEING A DAD. IN ONE OF MY DARKEST MOMENTS, HE HAD CONNECTED WITH ME IN A WAY I HAD LONGED FOR ALL MY LIFE.

of this, after all. I recognised that I had contributed to the hurt and disrespect dished out to women (Black women especially) by men (Black men). I understood that this change I was about to make was a process: a process that required time, patience, and accountability.

I returned to the UK with renewed energy and determination to work on myself. It would be eighteen months before I decided to get into another relationship. I felt I was not right for anyone. I knew I had a lot of work to do on myself, and while I did have a few casual encounters, I always made sure I was clear about my intentions. I knew I needed to fully understand myself and my childhood, and this was when I first sought out therapy. I didn't go into it expecting anything, I just knew I needed help to process all my feelings.

I have always had the capacity to overanalyse things, and this was the beginning of my love-hate relationship with the idea of any kind of therapy, simply because it shines a light on things you have long buried, and I don't like that. However, I have come to realise that to gain healing from anything, you have to deal with issues from the root. And this is exactly what happened. Psychotherapy really helped to streamline my thoughts. It enabled me to put things into perspective and, for the first time, I got to deal with things I thought I had forgotten. This was the first time I really got to understand my emotions. For example, I began to understand why I always got angry so quickly. This is no surprise, but I have learned that the thing with physical discipline – when it is the go-to method of correcting a child – is that it has a way of manifesting in the child's life as they get older. Often times the child (now an adult) responds to anything deemed as a threat with violence because they have been programmed into thinking this is the only way to resolve conflict — that violence is the only way to show dominance.

My first course of therapy lasted ten months. Even though I did not go back to it for a long time, I always knew I would return one day.

I started to develop myself spiritually. I started to pray again in addition to therapy, while also looking for work. I read a few books, like *The Alchemist* by Paulo Coelho, *The Seven Habits of Highly Effective People* by Stephen Covey, *Things Fall Apart* by Chinua Achebe, and my personal favourite, *The Subtle Art of Not Giving a F*ck* by Mark Manson. I started working out again — I picked up long-distance running — and most importantly I got to spend valuable time with Renae, just us alone in my new little space. For the first time, I got to really feel her and be there for her, my daughter.

At this time, I was living in a shared accommodation off East Street Market in south London. It was not cute to the eyes, but for me at that time it was perfect. A few weeks after my return to the UK, Mum visited. She came to ensure I was comfortable and took me to East Street Market to purchase basic things like pots, pans, cutlery, plates, and a red rug. I laugh now as I remember the rug. She spent a lot of time during that trip in the shared kitchen, cooking various meals to fill up my part of the fridge and freezer.

Shortly after Mum left, Dad visited. The first thing he did was buy me a bed because I was actually sleeping on the floor. But, like I said, none of this mattered too much. I had a roof over my head, I was focused on working on myself, I was trying to secure paid employment, and I was getting to spend time with Renae.

The part my parents played during this time was so important for my healing. I was a grown man, a father in my own right, but I got to see how things can be and how they should be. I got to see two individuals work together to ensure that their child was okay, and it filled me with strength and encouragement and kept me going. Maybe it also healed a childhood wound along the way.

I think this is a good place to talk about men's relationships with their spouses versus their relationships with their mothers.

During my relationship with Renae's mum, Sam, I will admit that I often put my mother first. I knew no better; she was my first love, after all, and she was the first person that really took the time to understand me and show me softness when I needed it the most. This often caused problems in my relationship with Sam, but I always thought she was overreacting – I mean this was my *mother,* how dare you think you can take her place?

The gag is, she was not trying to take Mum's place, she was only trying to establish hers. It took me a long time to realise that, though. It didn't even start to happen until I made that choice to take responsibility for the part I played in the breakdown of the relationship. I started to ask myself questions and follow up every answer with 'Why?' until I came to the conclusion that the way I felt about her actions, or reactions, was simply not reasonable. I mean, she'd said it a few times – she clearly stated she was not trying to compete with my mum – so why on earth did I feel that way? The answer was my insecurities and past trauma.

In her book *All About Love,* scholar and feminist bell hooks quotes John A Sandford, a psychoanalyst and priest:'As long as a man remains in a state of psychological development in which his mother is the most important woman to him, he cannot mature as a man. A man's eros, his capacity for love and relatedness, must be freed from attachment to the mother, and able to reach out to a woman who is his contemporary; otherwise he remains a demanding, dependent, childish person.'[3]

Sometimes – especially in extremely patriarchal societies where women are not valued by men – mothers can dote on their boy children, unconsciously searching for the connection in them that they are missing from the men who are present or absent from their lives. Because of this extra love and affection handed out to boy children, they can sometimes idealise their mothers, putting them on pedestals that all the other women in their lives must live up to. But this doesn't allow healthy relationships with other women and it can stunt the development of the men themselves, constantly having them in 'son' mode when they need to also be partners, husbands, or fathers.

A while ago, I was having a conversation with Mum and she said, 'Bodé, you are my everything. You are my father, my husband, my son, my brother, my confidant, my joy.' I responded by saying, 'Thank you, Mum, but I need you to understand that I am your son who may at times bring you joy and happiness. I am also happy for you to confide in me in certain cases, but I am not your husband, your father, your brother, and your everything. I am not your only child. My sisters – your daughters – are also part of you, which makes them part of your everything. I do not fancy all that responsibility. There are things your husband should provide that I will never be able to, so let us really be clear: I am someone else's husband and what I provide for her will not come to you or be for you.'

Let's just say, after this conversation, Mum did not speak to me for two weeks. She still sent me daily prayers and asked to speak to her grandkids, but it was obvious she was avoiding conversations with me. What I'd said didn't sit well with her at first, but it was the truth.

Even in so-called 'progressive' societies such as the UK, men can be fed the message that the only woman they can really trust is their mother. I'm not on Twitter, but I'm told of the debate that always ends up resurfacing, essentially boiling down to 'Who should men put first: their mother, their wife, the mother of their children, or their daughter?' Without a doubt, you will find someone arguing until they're sweating about how their mother must come above all. Not only is this a foolish debate, it is also potentially the result of something called 'enmeshment', where the emotional boundaries between a parent and child are compromised, and the child also becomes the parent's emotional caretaker. This is a type of 'parentification', which is basically when the roles of parent-child are reversed and a child ends up managing their parent in the way a parent should manage a child.

It sounds pretty serious, but boundaries can still be drawn, even if you've had that experience yourself. And if you want a healthy relationship with a significant other or your own children, those types of boundaries must be set.

It didn't happen overnight, but I have come to understand that both my mother and my partner have their place in my life, and a healthy, emotionally balanced life is one where they can and should exist simultaneously.

FATHERHOOD IN ACTION

I cannot overstate the important role that therapy has played in my life, especially with regards to unpacking childhood traumas. While it's good to have family and friends that you can talk to, impartial professional support can be vital, especially when dealing with some of the darker and more complicated parts of our experiences.

If you're in the UK, you can access free counselling through the NHS, either through a referral from your doctor or you can refer yourself on the NHS website.

Depending on what's available in your area, waiting times can be long, but the mental health charity Mind has advice on accessing free therapy from charities as well as directories for private therapists if you can afford it. Some therapists offer their prices on a sliding scale depending on your income.

The BAATN is a directory of Black and Asian therapists, which is helpful if you would like a therapist who may understand the nuances of your cultural background.

And finally, Black Minds Matter connects Black individuals and families with Black therapists free of charge.

You can find further resources on page 215.

CHAPTER 3

MASCULINITY & FATHERHOOD

"If the past cannot teach the present, and the father cannot teach the son, then history need not have bothered to go on, and the world has wasted a great deal of time."

– Russell Hoban

A lot of people think masculinity is under attack right now, but I disagree. I think that masculinity, in its current form, is coming to a reckoning. I believe that society has a problem – in fact, many problems – but one of them is that men do not really talk enough. They don't talk enough to each other, to friends, partners, family, or colleagues. At least, not in a meaningful way.

So what does it really mean to be a man today? If we look at how society generally defines being 'a man', it is to be strong, stoic, dominant, and secretive about how one truly feels. It is to be completely out of touch with one's emotions, even in situations where emotions absolutely cannot be ignored. I was listening to the radio station LBC the other day and Nick Ferrari was on air. The topic of discussion was the move by John Lewis to offer all of its 80,000-strong workforce six months of paid parental leave. Nick clearly did not agree with the move and even said, 'What father or man will want to take six months off to be with a newborn?' I was angry, and found myself shouting at the radio, saying, '*I* do!' I felt it was ludicrous that some men still think this way. I don't blame Nick though. After all, this is all he knows.

I have had my own experiences when it comes to parental leave. I remember when I wanted more than the usual two weeks off and my request was met with questions. I was asked why I wanted that and if it was necessary. I even had people tell me that the best place for me to be was at work, so I could give my other half enough time to bond with our newborn – because all I was going to do was be in her way and piss her off. I responded by saying, 'Is it wrong for me to also want to bond with our newborn? Is it wrong for me to want to share the responsibility that comes with dealing with a newborn? Is it wrong for me to want to change nappies and take part in night feeds – or is that also solely the woman's role?' Of course, I got no response to those questions other than, 'This is the way it is.' In the end though, I did get that time off – four weeks when RJ was born – and I bloody loved it.

But back to my initial point: I have often thought it is seen as empowering for women to express themselves around each other, whereas for men, it is seen as though we are giving away our power if we express ourselves among other men.

I grew up around a lot of women, and I am still surrounded by a lot of women. One thing I have realised is that they have an amazing ability to openly share how they truly feel. Prime example: as far as I know, my mother has always had the same group of friends. These women have, over the years, become mother figures to me. I can hear the table discussions, the laughing, the sly digs at husbands, comparing things their husbands did and did not do, the talks about careers and business, etc. My mother always left these get-togethers with a huge smile on her face, a smile backed up with renewed strength and confidence, and laced with the belief that everything was going to be okay – that she was not alone in her struggles as a woman in a country where women were often seen as 'just' women.

However, in the case of my dad and his friendship groups, all I saw were a bunch of alpha males.

I HAVE OFTEN THOUGHT IT IS SEEN AS EMPOWERING FOR WOMEN TO EXPRESS THEMSELVES AROUND EACH OTHER, WHEREAS FOR MEN, IT IS SEEN AS THOUGH WE ARE GIVING AWAY OUR POWER IF WE EXPRESS OURSELVES AMONG OTHER MEN.

I never thought they shared things with each other. In fact, what I saw was a lot of peacocking – who was trying to buy the most drinks or who had the loudest voice. Although I have no evidence of this, I am absolutely sure they never got themselves to a place where any one of them could be vulnerable with the others, for fear of being judged or classed as weak. I find this problematic.

My grandmother once said something to me. She said in Yoruba, '*Ishola* [the name she gave me], *inu e jin*.' In English, this basically means, 'You bottle things up. You don't share enough.' And boy, was she right. My hand could literally be on fire and I would be happy to continue keeping up appearances, acting like all is well.

This was exactly what happened when my relationship with Renae's mother was in the process of failing; I shared nothing with anyone. I told my parents and friends nothing. I felt ashamed to share, even though my whole world felt like it was crumbling. At the same time, I was going through disciplinary proceedings at my place of work, which led to me losing my job, as I mentioned earlier. This was disastrous because I really needed a job for my immigration status, but guess what I did? I kept that shit a secret. I woke up every day, got dressed, left the house, and acted as if I was going to work, even though I was only going to the nearby park to feed the ducks!

You see, this is the problem with the inability to share things. Everything that happened to me during that time was a recipe for disaster – disaster that could have been avoided if – and only if – I had spoken to someone and asked for help.

It all came out the day my mother decided to press hard and break through my defences — call it a mother's intuition. (That woman can tell if I have stubbed my toe just by hearing my voice on the phone!) She knew something was up and she knew I was hiding something. I had no choice. I had to let it all out and it felt absolutely freeing. I felt as though a weight had been lifted off my shoulders. I got the comfort I required, backed up with solutions afterwards.

Thinking back to that time, I now realise it would have been easier if I'd felt safe to speak to someone about what I was going through. The battle was both internal and external; my concept of 'being a man' was formed during my journey from boyhood to manhood — the impressions I gained from the men I grew up around, most notably my father, of course. I remember a time he was scolding me for crying and he said, 'No son of mine will grow up a sissy!' Back then, I didn't have the knowledge that I have now, and I remember how this felt. It hurt, and it definitely led to the toxic masculinity I went on to embody in my late teens and during early adulthood.

But the reality is, the masculinity I embodied at the time never even felt good in the first place! I was wearing a mask and pretending to be something that I thought I had to be, even though, ultimately, I was not. I tried with all my might to play that role with conviction, but that doesn't mean I didn't have questions. At the end of the day, you know when you're lying. You know when you're pretending to or deluding yourself. But I was talking myself into believing the image I was trying to portray. It didn't feel right, but I didn't know what else there was. I was already on a path I felt was inevitable, so I ran with it.

There was always an internal battle going on, and with that came a serious lack of confidence. Whenever I felt my persona was being questioned – it could be as small as someone asking why I did something – my back was up; I was overly defensive. I was desperately trying to hide my mask and stop it from slipping, but I knew that Sam, Renae's mum, could see right through my bullshit, and ironically that just made me amp up the defensiveness even more. I was caught in a lie and determined to run with it. No wonder our relationship broke down!

As I've said before, I was following a script laid out for me by my father. I have come to realise, by having my own children, that... Fatherhood. Is. Hard. And that is okay. It doesn't make me weak or less of a man because I feel this way. As a matter of fact, it makes me human. I have decided to be human. I guess my dad felt he wasn't allowed to be human, or that he had to be something else...

My father was strong and bold, the provider, the one whose word was final. He called the shots. He said jump and we asked how high. Although I resented it, I look back at those times and I understand his actions and behaviour. Truthfully, I hold nothing against him. This version of masculinity is all he knew. It was all he knew about how to parent, especially so with me, his first and only son. My father felt he had to be all those 'masculine' things to me and with me, that he had to show no weakness whatsoever because he did not want a 'weakling' as a son.

I think back to those moments when all I wanted was a hug, or maybe even some recognition for the good work I'd done, such as getting an amazing school report, which happened a lot. I somehow absorbed the lack of celebration I received from my dad. I shoved my old school reports into an envelope and left it in the back of a cupboard at the house Candice and I lived in in Croydon a while ago. One day Candice's mum came round and she discovered the envelope with all my certificates from primary and high school.

Candice and her mum were both shocked at what they saw. Candice's mum dropped the envelope on the table when I came home from work that day. She said, 'Bodé, I didn't realise you were this smart! I found this behind the linen and, wow – so many "A"s!' I just shrugged as if it didn't matter, and Candice and her mum were both startled at my response. I now make a point of celebrating everything with my children. I feel it is important to instil pride for their achievements. I am trying to break the cycle, after all.

And when it comes to birthdays… quick secret: I did not celebrate them until recently, and it is still a struggle because I get overwhelmed by the attention. I learned the act of not highlighting or celebrating birthdays because, again, it was not something that was done while I was growing up. Of course, I saw friends and peers being celebrated for their birthdays, but in our household, for some reason – and I still don't have an answer for it – it was not celebrated. Maybe I would get the odd 'happy birthday' or prayer in the morning, but it was treated as any other day.

That is why, when my twenty-first birthday came along – I was in the UK by this time – my aunty decided to do something big for me. She got a cake and a camera and even invited a few people. Mum was in the country too. There was food and drinks, but that day was a blur to me. I was present and at the same time absent – it felt pretty weird. I was forced to put on something a bit fancy for the photos and, on the whole, that birthday celebration was a forced one. I remember turning up to a nightclub at the Hilton hotel in Paddington. A friend had found out we shared the same birthday and she told me she'd made a booking at the club for both of us – that we should both bring our friends to celebrate. I turned up at the club with no friends – can you imagine? *No friends!* – while she, on the other hand, had a lot of people around her. It highlighted the fact that I was there alone.

I made the mistake of mentioning this during a therapy session and as always, my therapist was all over it. She wasn't going to let go even though I continued to insist, right there in the therapy session, that it was okay. But my therapist helped me understand that I had grown used to a lack of celebration, and this made perfect sense. It allowed me to really assess how I act at Christmas and the kids' birthdays. I am most definitely doing better at celebrating their special occasions nowadays. I won't let them internalise the messages I did as a child – that celebration is not important, that nothing I did was enough, it was always B+, must do better.

This lack of celebration I experienced as a child also extended to a lack of displays of affection. And it went beyond special days and school achievements.

Even now, I still feel weird any time Dad tries to give me a hug because I have grown used to the absence of them. I learned to live without them, which basically meant I learned to live without what – I now believe – I needed most as a child.

When I look back at those times, I realise that my relationship with my father was one that was filled with fear. This does not mean I did not (and do not) love and respect him, but instilling fear was always the order of the day. I used to dread when my dad would return from work, to the point that whenever I heard the engine of his vehicle, I would make myself disappear. I knew full well that if I had not completed my homework or finished feeding our dogs – we had three massive Germans shepherds, called Prince, Princess, and Caesar – all hell would break loose. As a child, every night while alone in my bedroom, I would dream of the day that I no longer needed to answer to or take direction from him, the day I would have my own space and be old enough to do whatever the hell I wanted.

Still, I definitely learned to be the guy he wanted me to be. You know, that strong, stoic, without-feelings guy? Yup, that was me fifteen years ago, and that was me when Renae was born – I was toxic AF.

I admire a few men and one notable one is the actor Will Smith. He has spoken openly about his upbringing with a father who was in the military, and he has gone on to talk about how he too embodied this way of being 'a man' early on in his fatherhood journey. Will Smith talks about how he got it completely wrong with his first son and wrong again with his second, but how things changed when his daughter came along.

FATHERHOOD. IS. HARD. AND THAT IS OKAY

He realised through her questions, and most especially when she decided to quit her music career, that he was essentially continuing what he'd experienced as a child and projecting it on to his kids. I understand where he is coming from. I made a decision early on, when my second child, Esmé, was born, that I would parent differently. In the film *Fatherhood*, actor Kevin Hart plays a new father named Matthew Logelin. He uses what I think is the perfect phrase: 'Through my father's actions, I learned how not to be a father.'[4] I believe when you get to that point in your fatherhood journey where you are self-reflective and self-aware, you are automatically on the right track.

The clash between my parenting style and that of my dad's is still evident in some ways. 'Why are you changing the nappy? Why can't Candice do it?' Dad asked when he was visiting after the birth of my third child, RJ. I sighed. I knew exactly what he was trying to say and I also knew this was a teachable moment. I didn't even realise the words were coming out, but I responded (admittedly loaded with a bit of salt), 'Dad, he is my child also.'

Dad got the message immediately, and I know this because of what he said next: 'It is impressive that you know how to change a baby's nappy. I never did it with you guys and I regret it.' I saw this as an opportunity to have further conversations around his parenting, so I responded by saying, 'Well, there's a lot more you could have done differently.'

I was met with a confused look on his face, but I continued. The confidence to do this definitely came from the work I was doing in therapy – I was

WHEN YOU GET TO THAT POINT IN YOUR FATHERHOOD JOURNEY WHERE YOU ARE SELF-REFLECTIVE AND SELF-AWARE, YOU ARE AUTOMATICALLY ON THE RIGHT TRACK.

emboldened, and there was a bit of anger, perhaps, and frustration, when I said, 'Dad, you were strict, and I have to be honest, I sometimes felt unloved by you. I always felt I couldn't have a conversation with you without fear of being shouted at.' The next thing Dad did shocked me. He apologised. He said, 'I am sorry I brought you up as a scared man. I grew up surrounded by the failure of my brothers to make anything of themselves, and I did not want my son to fail. In doing so, I failed in some ways as your father. You did need the strict hand sometimes though, but I feel I went over the top most of the time. I look at you now and conclude that you are a better father than I ever was. I never imagined that you, Bodé, would grow up to be a father like this. I am learning how to be a parent once again from you, my son. I respect you. I respect what you are doing, how you are doing it, and who you have become.'

I was gobsmacked. All of a sudden, I felt myself get really close to tears. I remained silent. My mind was racing. Most importantly, a connection was established with Dad in that very moment. In my head though, I kept repeating to myself, 'I will ensure my children never feel like this.'

In that moment, I got to know Dad like I have never done before. I got an insight into who he was and what he experienced growing up. It made perfect sense, of course. I mean, why hadn't I ever thought about him as a child before?

My friends and I often have conversations about parenting and how difficult it can be, especially as most of them are also navigating the traumas experienced while growing up. Only a small fraction of my friends think the same way as I do. The others don't, and this is understandable — we are all at different stages of development and of our journeys.

Some believe that the way most of us grew up was necessary. One in particular feels he deserved the treatment he got, and that that is the reason why he turned out good — which means he will most certainly bring up his children in the same way.

My friends had varied childhood experiences. Two of them are stuck in the 'old' version of masculinity. They think being an alpha male is the only way to live, and it shows every time we speak or have open debate on such topics. They make statements like, 'I can never allow my wife to earn more than me!' My issue is with the word 'allow'. It sounds as if they see themselves as the gatekeeper to the success or any kind of advancement of their significant other, and it is damn near impossible to get them to see things another way.

I believe that, even in this day and age, the number of men who think this way far outnumbers those that do not. I also think it is safe to say their upbringing (either their parents or their environment) plays a major part in the way they think.

But I believe we need a new vision of masculinity, and that this new vision will change how we approach fatherhood. I firmly believe that men need to learn to embrace what can be described as 'feminine energy'.

We all have both 'masculine' and 'feminine' energy. Men have been pre-programmed to focus on the masculine energy. I think masculine energy is generally considered as being strong, stable, and self-confident.

Making decisions fast; being decisive. Knowing what you want and going after it with purpose and direction. The world has been built on masculine energy. We are told that to be something in life, you need to embody masculine energy. Women are told they need to embrace it to succeed in the workplace. (Though they are often penalised for it by being perceived as a 'bitch' whereas a man showing the same qualities would just be seen as assertive – but that's a whole other conversation.)

But for men to start to understand and connect with themselves, their partner, their children, and the world at large, they need to draw on 'feminine energy' too. Feminine energy is often identified as empathy, listening more, and being in touch with your own emotions. I believe it's important for children to see that 'feminine energy' is as equally important as 'masculine energy' – especially for boys who will grow up to be the next generation of men. We can and should break those stereotypes. And this is relevant whether a man is in a relationship with a woman or another man because queer relationships can definitely be just as toxic as heterosexual ones.

IT'S IMPORTANT FOR CHILDREN TO SEE THAT 'FEMININE ENERGY' IS AS EQUALLY IMPORTANT AS 'MASCULINE ENERGY' – ESPECIALLY FOR BOYS WHO WILL GROW UP TO BE THE NEXT GENERATION OF MEN.

FATHERHOOD IN ACTION

It takes a lot of work to reframe masculinity and femininity as characteristics that are not gendered but simply very different. It is a whole new way of looking at the world. But just because it's a lot of work doesn't mean you shouldn't start small. Here are some simple ways to break out of your pre-programmed desire to embody masculine energy.

Define what a man should be in today's world

Remember, the world no longer needs men who are intolerant, abusive, and corrupt. We need men who are conscious of their actions, men who shine, men who have realised that the many myths about men and women they have absorbed are false. Men who are powerful and kind, focused and creative. Warm-hearted and driven. Firm and tolerant. A strong man is a man who is conscious of all parts of himself, including his feminine energy.

Tap in to feminine energy

Feminine energy is the energy of life. It's the energy of being, not doing. Bright side traits of feminine energy include creativity, being in the flow, intuition, nurturing, listening, love, openness, empathy, and the expression of feelings.

Deconstruct myths

We are brainwashed by the norms of the society we are born into, inheriting whatever belief systems come with it. Genetics can also shape our world view. Current research in behavioural epigenetics indicates that past trauma – whether our own, or that of our ancestors – leaves molecular scars that attach to our DNA. We inherit not only physical characteristics but also the behavioural and psychological tendencies of our ancestors.[5] These myths are programmed into us, including:

- Crying is for females.

- Men must be stoic and shy away from expression of emotion.

- Men must be successful in their career.

- A man is the head of the household.

- Men are primarily left-brain- and logic-oriented.

- Men must dominate women, physically, financially, and sexually.

- Men must be aggressively self-confident.

These myths can only be unlearned with conscious effort and participation on our parts.

CHAPTER 4

FATHERING

"The nature of impending fatherhood is that you are doing something that you're unqualified to do, and then you become qualified while doing it."

– John Green

I read something great written in a leaflet handed out by the National Fatherhood Initiative, an American research organisation that works around father involvement and engagement. It said, 'Fathering isn't the same thing as parenting. "Fathering" is your unique ability to contribute to the good health and well-being of your children and family. "Parenting" is the knowledge and skills that dads and mums need to raise healthy, happy children.'[6]

Your position as a father is unique, regardless of how you become one. One very important point to say from the beginning is that you are more than a pay cheque. Fathering involves supporting your children in *all* the ways they need you and caring for their physical, emotional, intellectual, and spiritual needs.

I was always the thinker for as long as I can remember, and oftentimes I was deep in my thoughts, questioning what other people just see as the way of life, religion, or tradition. My grandmother referred to me being a thinker when she was telling me off for not sharing enough, whereas Dad saw this as me being two-faced. He felt that his male child should be boisterous and extroverted, not introverted as I was, which often confused me. Any time I was home – an environment where I felt caged, choked up – I found myself exploring my deepest thoughts again. The elders called this daydreaming, as if that was a bad thing, but I disagreed then and still disagree now. The daydreaming they so disapproved of was an escape for me. It provided an environment where I could let my mind run free. I believe having that is important for children and even adults because in that land of daydreams anything is possible.

I would say I have mastered the art of daydreaming. Nowadays, any time I am faced with a challenge, I don't stress over it. I go to sleep, knowing full well that when I wake up, I will have an idea or a solution because somehow my subconscious mind evaluates all possible scenarios, providing me with a way out. It is because of this that I encourage my children to dream, to let their imaginations run free. Because in my opinion, that is where anything is possible. Right there, logic is formed without the influence of societal norms. External pressures we experience in everyday life no longer exist. I was discussing this with my therapist once and she gave me a perfect name for this. She called it an 'out of body experience'. When I daydream, I am able to stand outside of myself to look at all available outcomes and scenarios. I become a spectator in my own spectacle, and this provides a wider view, allowing me to see what I may not see when I am laser-focused on a situation.

And there are times when the answer simply won't come. I think a lot about the idea of comfort versus solutions. There are situations when all that is required is the comfort of knowing it's okay not to have all the answers. Accepting that fact reduces the focus on perfection and, after all, no one is truly perfect!

Therapy has really helped me understand a few things about my childhood – things I thought I had long forgotten about. I didn't realise they were always there in the background, manifesting in other ways. The most important thing therapy has done for me though, is that it's helped me understand this: most of us come from a place of what we know – you are only able to give from what you have.

The only 'fathering' I knew was what I'd seen from my own father: a style that was strict, macho, and what we now describe as 'toxic masculinity', where cultural pressures cause men to behave in a certain way. Amy Morin, psychologist and editor-in-chief of the mental health website *Verywell Mind* defines toxic masculinity as 'the notion that some people's idea of "manliness" perpetuates domination, homophobia, and aggression; the idea that men need to act tough and avoid showing all emotions.'[7]

There was no room for my feelings or ideas as a child. I had to do what I was told and show no weakness whatsoever. This is why, when I visualised my own version of fatherhood early on, I decided I would do the opposite of what I had been shown. I looked back at my time as a child and remembered how I just wanted an emotional connection and it didn't happen.

Despite the differences in our perspectives, there is a lot of empathy from me towards Dad. Through therapy, I have come to understand that transgenerational trauma does exist and this is what was manifesting. According to the mental health resource website, Goodtherapy.org, transgenerational trauma is 'trauma that gets passed down from those who directly experience an incident to subsequent generations.'[8]

To better understand this, let's look at physical discipline as an example, especially within Black communities. Let's be honest, physical discipline – how it is practised within Black communities – is directly linked to slavery. Violent ideas like 'breaking the buck' (where enslaved men were punished for their defiance) were bound to leave lasting effects on generations to come. (I speak more on this in chapter 7.) Understanding these links from one generation to the next has helped me deal with my trauma and cut it out because I sure as hell don't want to pass any trauma on to my children.

Even though I don't necessarily see my Dad as my fathering role model, there are still times when he surprises me. I was on the phone with him recently and, during that call, Renae called me. I hung up from the call with Dad to have a little chat with Renae about the second laptop she had somehow broken in the space of a year. Of course, I was upset about this and I let her know that. She understood and I told her I will give her a call later. I called Dad back and he knew instantly that I was a bit pissed off, so he asked what happened. I just exploded, telling him how I was so upset because Renae seemed to lack an understanding about the value of things. He was quiet throughout my rant and after, there was a long pause from him. He seemed to be taking it all in. This is when something special happened. Over the years, we'd had a few small discussions about how he brought me up, but what I didn't know was that he saw this moment on the phone as an opportunity to accept and confirm things that I already knew and struggled with.

UNDERSTANDING THESE LINKS FROM ONE GENERATION TO THE NEXT HAS HELPED ME DEAL WITH MY TRAUMA AND CUT IT OUT BECAUSE I SURE AS HELL DON'T WANT TO PASS ANY TRAUMA ON TO MY CHILDREN.

He started by saying, 'Bodé, I need you to understand one thing, and that is the fact that she is a child and this is what kids do. Yes, I know it is annoying, especially since the laptops were not cheap and you only just bought her a new one at Christmas, but I need you to understand that the saying, "spare the rod, spoil the child," is not correct. With children you need to spare the rod, always.'

At this point you could have literally picked my jaw up off the floor. He continued, 'But there are times when you have to correct the child, but mostly you just need to give them a cuddle and make them understand the importance of things. I wish I did this with you. I know every time I try to hug you now, it feels weird to you. I feel you physically pull away from the hug as if you are ashamed or scared of it.'

He went on to say, 'If you deal with your child based on fear, you will never get them to open up and be free with you. Imagine a situation where she is scared of you. Then the laptop breaks and she decides to hide it from you, and then looks for other means, that you are not okay with, to fix the laptop because she does not want to be told off by you. I know this happened several times with us. You were never free with me. You hid things from me, which affected you growing up, and I must admit it is a miracle that you have turned out the way you are.'

I was silent. I was silent because I was in shock. I was silent not because I didn't like what I was hearing, but because I was finally hearing it. It felt so surreal. I felt my body get so light and I felt light-headed, as if I was experiencing the biggest kind of high. I felt dizzy, which was immediately followed by tears falling from my eyes.

Dad did not stop there. 'I am going to tell you a story about my upbringing.'

He told me that when he was growing up, his mother – my grandmother, who I never got to meet because she died before my birth – was the breadwinner in the family. That was really hard on his dad – my grandfather – especially during that period in time.

Dad was born in 1955, and Nigeria gained its independence from the British in 1960. Even now, Nigeria is quite a patriarchal society. Power is mostly held by men and cultural norms all favour men. One can only imagine what it was like back then, when Dad was growing up. According to Dad, Grandpa faced a lot of ridicule from his peers, which caused resentment in the household. Apparently, Grandpa was quite vocal about his dislike of Grandma's success. It made him feel less of a man because he had to rely on a woman.

But Dad idolised his father, and this is quite clear from the way he speaks about the man, whom he clearly believes was unappreciated and treated unfairly.

Learning about the dynamics of my grandparents' relationship, I have come to understand that this is what forms the basis of Dad's masculinity. He believes being masculine is to never appear vulnerable or weak. It is as if he really overcompensates by ensuring he is always in control.

For Dad, growing up in a household where the woman was the breadwinner could not have been easy. I imagine he would have witnessed first-hand the snide comments and ridicule dished out to his dad from other men in the community. He would have also witnessed certain actions from his dad towards his mum, which I have no doubt

SPARE THE ROD, ALWAYS

were absolutely toxic. But that was what he knew. That is what he drew on when he became a father.

Dad tried so hard to make me be like him. I imagine he felt that if it was good for him then it would automatically be good for me – but the idea of 'good' is highly subjective. How often do we see situations as good for us, when really it's just something we have learned to live with? We've turned out okay, so we believe the way we got here was necessary. I wholeheartedly disagree with this. If we don't deal with the traumatic episodes from our past, they will always manifest into something else in the future. We need to deal with them in healthy ways (therapy, for example), so we can avoid projecting past traumas onto others.

While I do respect my dad and the part he played and continues to play in my life (now more than ever), my fatherhood role model is Will Smith, as I mentioned in the previous chapter. I have followed Will Smith's journey, especially regarding fatherhood. During one of the many conversations with his wife, Jada Pinkett Smith, on the *Red Table Talk* TV show, they said something that really struck me, which was that parents sometimes see their children as possessions instead of separate beings who have their own journeys and paths in the world.

This idea really resonated with me. I had always felt that my children are their own people, with their own feelings, journeys, and destinies. I am just a vessel to help guide them. I don't want to squeeze out their individuality based around my own fears and experience, because those are unique to me. And it is most certainly not a one-size-fits-all task; all children are different, even if they are from the same household, parents, and womb. My children have most certainly shown me this and I have received that message because I make sure I am present, physically and emotionally, so I am able to really feel them.

RJ loves his own space and boundaries, even though he is only three right now. He is happy to be by himself in his room, playing with Duplo. When he wants to construct a bridge, he prefers to do it how he wants, even if it means it is upside down.

Now that I'm a father, I try to keep the past and all the inherited trauma out of it. I look at my children and try to father each of them individually. My fathering philosophy is based on an authoritative approach to parenting. This means that I am all about setting expectations – and providing the resources my kids need to meet them. I am a big believer in boundaries and consequences, but I know there's a grey area as well, so I always try to show my kids that the why behind something matters a lot.

My approach is – what I think – a perfect blend of authoritarian and permissive, meaning I set expectations while being warm and nurturing. I am clear with my children that there will be consequences for bad behaviour – and I will most certainly follow through on them.

There is a big difference between being an authoritative and authoritarian parent. Dad was the latter, in that his kids were expected to obey without question. On the flip side, I'd much rather my children ask questions about what I ask of them. I want them to try to understand the reasoning behind discipline and consequences. After all, isn't that the only way they'll actually learn from their mistakes?

For example, I wouldn't just send any of my children to time-out. Instead, I might join them for the time-out or help them reason through their actions so they learn, not only that whatever it is that they've done isn't okay, but also how to problem-solve the same scenario next time.

I find this to be a very balanced approach to parenting because it teaches responsibility and how to make good choices, but it also helps foster independence. The bottom line for me is to follow through on discipline, but always with the endgame of teaching my kids how to navigate conflict down the road.

FATHERHOOD IN ACTION

Unpacking and dealing with our transgenerational trauma and the fathering toolkit inherited from our fathers or father figures, present or absent, is an absolute necessity. Here are a few things we can all do.

Acceptance

As with almost anything of this nature, one must first accept that there is an issue. I am of the school of thought that we all suffer from some sort of trauma.

Seeking Help

This is not the kind of thing to sort out by yourself. This is not the time to carry the world on your shoulders like you think you need to, like you think others assume of you. You are allowed to be vulnerable and seek help.

Therapy

This follows on from my point above about seeking help. Therapy is the first place to start. You need someone who is skilled in this area to help unpack those things you may not even realise are present. A good psychotherapist will help with understanding and defining traumatic experiences. See the end of chapter 2 and further resources on page 215 for advice on finding a therapist.

Self-Reflection

It's one thing to know there is an issue and what the issue is, but actually taking steps to ensure you identify situations where you may be toxic is another. The art of self-reflection is like looking into a mirror and describing what you see. It is a way of assessing yourself. This can provide an opportunity to see things from the eyes of your inner child. It will allow you to start asking the right questions like, 'How did I feel when my parents did this to me?' and 'If I didn't like it, what makes me think it is right and that my child is okay with it?'

CHAPTER 5

CHILD DEVELOPMENT

"To take children seriously is to value them for who they are right now rather than as adults-in-the-making."

— Alfie Kohn

Every culture around the world has different ideas about child development – or how to raise your kids – that are embedded within it. A lot of these ideas revolve around the cultural values of the community you come from. I read an interview in *The Atlantic*, with Robert and Sarah LeVine, a married anthropologist and researcher who have spent more than five decades researching child rearing in different cultures around the world. They speak about the different parenting styles they've witnessed in countries as varied as Japan, Kenya, Nepal, Denmark and, of course, America. 'Parents in every culture at a given moment think they're doing the optimal thing for their kids. But their concept of what is optimal is extremely different from another culture and even from another generation in their own culture,' says Robert LeVine.[9]

There's a whole industry making a lot of money telling us how to raise our kids. You could even say this book I'm writing is part of that, but the LeVines have found, through their research, that there isn't one single way to raise children that can be seen as the 'best' or the 'most successful'. We're all out here trying our best, right?

It's probably kind of a cliché to say, but my children have taught me a lot! Parenting three different children, with three different personalities, sometimes feels like a constant game of gymnastics. What I've come to understand, and what I truly believe, is that each child needs to be parented differently – and, believe it or not, your kids will teach you how to parent them. Don't believe me? Bear with me and let me explain.

As you've already heard by now, when I was a kid, there was only one way – and more often than not, it was my dad's way. Dad was overpowering and had a strong idea of what he wanted and expected for each of his children. When I was a young boy, I was quite the athlete. I even had a sub-eleven-second time on the 100-metre sprint. The possibility of becoming a professional athlete and putting my talent to good use excited me, but Dad said no. The plan was that I was going to go to university to study economics. No ifs, buts, or maybes. Even though I was young, I knew exactly what was going on – I didn't have a voice and my feelings didn't matter.

Due to my own experiences as a child, I knew that when it came to my kids, I wanted to – had to – do things differently. I wanted to be the parent who listened and paid attention to what they were saying, and sometimes, more crucially, what they were not saying. In doing this, I've had to have patience with them, and myself, as I've learned to deconstruct and reconstruct what I've thought about myself and what I experienced during childhood. A lot of this has been done in therapy – learning how to unlock the emotions I've hidden away for so long. I watch my children express emotions similar to those I felt as a child, but which I didn't have the space to express for myself. One thing I recognise in my children, is that, like me, they are each sensitive in their own way. I wasn't necessarily always given the space to be sensitive and express that sensitivity as a child, so a big part of my approach to parenting is giving them the opportunity and a safe space to freely express themselves in full.

In recognising their differences, however, I know that they will need different things to prepare themselves for the world. For example, while Esmé's siblings, Renae and RJ, are very good at focusing on themselves and asserting boundaries, Esmé intuitively considers other people's feelings before she thinks of her own. This makes her very empathetic and a kind soul who always wants to help. When Candice and I went on our honeymoon recently, she missed us a lot, but refused to tell us when we FaceTimed her. She didn't want us to worry while we were away, almost punishing herself for our sake. In this, she is very similar to me and my personality and, while I don't want to change her, I do worry sometimes about what this means for her as she grows up. There are those who will want to take advantage of her nature for their own benefit. I'm often thinking about how I can guide her through that, so she is strong and assertive, while still maintaining her empathy and soft heart towards others.

I think sometimes as parents, because we're around our kids every single day and are often fighting for

EACH CHILD NEEDS TO BE PARENTED DIFFERENTLY

alone time or for a moment to get our thoughts in order, we think that we know our kids by default. But reflecting on my childhood, I know a big part of my emotional disconnection from my dad was feeling like he didn't really know me, even though we were in each other's faces almost every day.

Letting your kids 'teach' you how to parent them is essentially just paying a lot of attention to them, noticing their personality, their needs, their quirks, and their insecurities. It is about seeing where they excel and are confident, and where they need a bit of encouragement or guidance.

Similarly, there is perhaps a larger than average age gap between my children, and this also brings different needs and desires — especially when it comes to spending time with me. Renae and Esmé don't always want to be around their dad, but when RJ wants Daddy-time, I know that I have to respond immediately because if I tell him to 'wait a minute', by the time I'm ready to sit down and watch *Paw Patrol* with him, he's moved on to something else. Sometimes he's not even watching his show anymore, but as long as he knows I'm there, and he can rest his leg on top of mine, he's good.

With the older girls, I have to request that one-on-one time. Sometimes it might be a trip to the shops, followed by a meal and some conversation, or something as simple as sitting down at the kitchen table with a muffin. With Esmé, we have a lot of similar interests, including geography, the solar system, and Formula 1, so much of our bonding time is around our shared interests. With Renae, however,

LETTING YOUR KIDS 'TEACH' YOU HOW TO PARENT THEM IS ESSENTIALLY JUST PAYING A LOT OF ATTENTION TO THEM, NOTICING THEIR PERSONALITY, THEIR NEEDS, THEIR QUIRKS, AND THEIR INSECURITIES.

she's at the age where our conversation is less general chit-chat and more focused on boys, relationships, education, or her potential career paths. It's all about connecting in the right way at the right time.

FATHERHOOD IN ACTION

I am always learning and questioning things as my kids grow. By continuing to focus on their individual needs, I hope and pray to be a strong support for their development. When you think about making moves to spend quality time with your child or children, it can be helpful to keep the below in mind.

- What does each child like to do – especially when they are alone?

- My favourite pastime with RJ is to play with Duplo blocks. He loves this and I let him lead here. Often, when he is alone in his room, you will find him constructing various items with bits of Duplo.

- What do they talk about with their friends?

- Children are always communicating with us through words and body language. If you watch and listen closely enough, you can figure out what interests your child from the conversations they have. Ask about what they discuss with their friends. This was how I found out that

Esmé is really into her super cars – because she would often mention the cars she and her friends chatted about in school.

- What do they need from their parents at this stage?

- Children are good at communicating what they require from us. It is up to us to pay attention to said request and try not to enforce our own thought processes on them.

CHAPTER 6

RAISING BOYS, RAISING GIRLS

"We've begun to raise daughters more like sons... but few have the courage to raise our sons more like our daughters."

– Gloria Steinem

I want to start this chapter by telling a story.

The birth experience of Esmé is one episode I am not sure I will ever be able to get over. In the spirit of honesty, I must admit that even though, at the time of writing, she is eight, I still suffer from serious guilt because I don't feel I ever got the opportunity to bond with her the way I would have loved to in the first six months of her life. There is so much trauma to unpack – and hopefully I'll get to deal with this in therapy one day – because I somehow feel that maybe I should have done more. Maybe I should have been harder on the doctors, nurses, and midwives. Maybe I should have asked more questions and maybe I shouldn't have left at that crucial moment to have a shower…

When we found out that Candice was pregnant with our first child together, we were filled with so much joy. We felt this was going to be the moment when our relationship would be given much needed recognition by the people around us. We were two individuals deep into our journeys of self-discovery and, in some ways, we were looking for external validation and to be taken seriously as a couple. So, when we found out we had a baby on the way, we started to prepare in the ways we knew how – Candice in her way, and me in mine.

I was still at the early stages of my career then and spending a lot of time at work, which meant Candice went to a lot of the hospital appointments alone. She always called me afterwards and we had further conversations when I returned home. Whilst the conversations filled me with lots of joy, I always felt a certain anger when she mentioned how she was treated by the hospital staff. There were constant judgements, snide comments, and assumptions every time she attended her appointments. The assumption was that I, the father, was absent, and that she was a single mother with no one to support her. One nurse even said boldly to her one day, 'I am assuming no husband?'

What did I expect? Society will have you believing the narrative of the absent Black father, and this cannot be further away from the truth. The stereotype of Black fathers as 'absent' and Black children as 'fatherless' – which first surfaced more than fifty years ago – has, like many racial stereotypes, refused to die.

In 1965, white sociologist and Assistant Secretary of Labour, Daniel Patrick Moynihan, published a report called *The Negro Family: The Case For National Action*. This report claimed that increasing rates of 'out-of-wedlock' births and single-mother homes among African Americans signalled the coming destruction of Black families, and that these trends were to blame for many of the issues facing the Black community in America.[10]

The report has since been criticised by many race scholars[11], yet even Black public figures have shared statistics from it. In 2008, President Barack Obama said during his Father's Day speech that 'more than half of

SOCIETY WILL HAVE YOU BELIEVING THE NARRATIVE OF THE ABSENT BLACK FATHER, AND THIS CANNOT BE FURTHER AWAY FROM THE TRUTH.

all Black children live in single-parent households… Children who grow up without a father are five times more likely to live in poverty and commit crime; nine times more likely to drop out of school; and twenty times more likely to end up in prison. They are more likely to have behavioural problems or run away from home or become teenage parents themselves. And the foundations of our community are weaker because of it.'[12]

This stereotype ignores clear evidence that Black fathers are, in fact, more involved in their children's care and their lives, than fathers of other races. For starters, we cannot equate the number of unmarried dads to the number of 'fatherless' children. Marriage rates don't necessarily reflect the number of Black fathers living with their children. As writer Josh Levs points out, the majority of Black dads (2.5 million out of around 4.2 million) do live with their kids, even if they're not married to their partner.[13] And second of all, according to a 2013 US National Health Statistics report, Black dads – whether they live with their children or not – are more actively involved in their children's lives than their counterparts of other races.

For example, the report states that Black fathers who live with their children are more likely than fathers of other races to provide physical care (bathing, changing nappies, feeding) for their young children, read to their children, and help their children with their homework – all on a daily basis – than fathers of other races who also cohabit with their kids.

The report also reveals that, among dads who don't live with their children, Black dads are more likely to be involved in care, including reading to their children, helping them with homework, talking to them about their days, and taking them to activities, than Hispanic or white dads who live apart from their kids. Non-residential Black fathers are also the least likely to report that they're not at all involved in the care of their children.[14]

These are figures for the US alone and I can say the same for Nigeria where I am from and grew up. I can categorically say that around 95 per cent of the homes I visited had present fathers.

Getting back to Candice telling me about her hospital appointments. 'Yes, we are not married, but for fuck's sake!' I said once as Candice told what had happened that day. 'Why do these people always do this? How the hell is it his business?' (Yes, it was a guy.)

'What does being married have to do with your check-up? Do you get better treatment if you are married – or is he assuming that I'm in jail or that you got impregnated by someone who's dead now?'

While at first I was unable to make it to a lot of those appointments, I realised from early on – based on Candice's narration of her experiences at those appointments – that I had to be a support. This was going to be a long journey and I had to make sure I was there, providing a shoulder to lean on.

Sadly, it didn't get better as the pregnancy went on. Our baby was overdue and we had to go to hospital once again for Candice to be induced. For three days, Candice was examined, pricked, and prodded, and each time this happened, the nurses and midwives acted as if I did not exist. They simply looked past me, ignored me, and spoke amongst themselves, talking in hushed tones and quiet voices. I started to feel useless, and on the fourth day I had had enough. As the midwife approached to carry out observations once again, I threw questions at her. I needed to know what the hell was going on and why I was being kept in the dark. I needed to know why Candice was being treated as if she was by herself.

I could tell instantly that the midwife did not like that. She said that according to her notes, Candice was there alone, even though I had been there, by her side, every day for four days straight, only leaving when I needed to get some food or a change of clothing. But anyways, I insisted on knowing what was going on. I wanted to know what medication they were administering so I could jump on Google to research and respond with questions on possible side effects and the plan of action.

Later on that day, I decided to go home briefly for a quick shower and to get some supplies. The moment I got home I got a phone call from Candice, saying her waters had been broken. I was livid because once again the staff at the hospital decided to treat her as if she were alone. I had specifically told them before I left to hold off on any treatment until I returned.

Esmé was finally born after eighteen hours of induced labour, but this is when the real trouble began. The whole experience was hard on us but, for some reason, the hospital staff thought it necessary to inform child services about a perceived threat to the life of our child. I have no idea why, but the staff told child services that Candice was there all alone and could possibly harm our child – which was totally absurd and unacceptable. Candice had just faced what I could classify the most traumatic thing she'd ever experienced. This is a woman who had prepared herself mentally and physically for the arrival of our child, and the staff completely misrepresented her here. And their actions totally ignored the fact that I, the father of the child, had been there every step of the way.

I was invited to a meeting — an 'investigation' they called it — at the child services facility in Croydon to prove that I was indeed the father and that I had been involved every step of the way. This was really painful. They then requested to visit our house to ensure we were bringing our child home to a safe environment. After the successful visit to our house, they asked me to sign an agreement that Esmé was going to be released to me and not Candice. It was so insulting and painful. All of this was really mind-blowing but at that point we did not have the strength or time to fight anything; we just wanted our child home with us.

You would think it was all going to end there, but you would be mistaken. Two days after we returned home, Candice started to feel pretty rough. Two midwives visited during that time and when we explained what was going on, they put it down to her body, ridding itself of all the pregnancy water. While Candice felt unwell, I found myself taking on multiple roles. I was Mummy and Daddy, running on little or no sleep. Even though there was a lot going on, Esmé needed to be looked after.

A few days later, it turned out that Candice was experiencing the early stages of sepsis and had to be taken to hospital for emergency surgery. So there I was, dealing with the possibility of becoming a single dad, and I was terrified. Let us bear in mind that (at the time of writing this book) Black women in the UK are four to five times more like to die during childbirth, as stated in the 2021 MBRRACE-UK report,[15] so I am sure you can understand why I was thinking this way. The experience in itself was traumatic and one I would never want to revisit ever again.

With Candice in hospital, looking after Esmé was all on me. Following her surgery, Candice slowly recovered but for two weeks, looking after Esmé was all on me. All I had to key in to or refer to was the training I had received from Mum. And all I could remember were the times Mum had me in the kitchen instead of my sisters, those times Mum had me cleaning instead of my sisters. This is the foundation of my parenting style and, in our household, we do not subscribe to society's definition of gender roles.

You often hear that with boys you have to take a 'rougher' approach, so to speak, because apparently boys need to be tougher. You often hear that boys shouldn't cry and that they need to be more masculine. People even go so far as to ask questions like, 'Why are you crying like a little girl?' I have a few friends who were never allowed in the kitchen while growing up because they were male. Girls, on the other hand, are treated softly and forced to wear colours deemed feminine, for example, pink.

Ultimately, we want our kids to be equipped for life, right? We don't want our sons to starve or live in a filthy house, and we don't want our daughters to be less confident or allow themselves to be bossed around. What we teach our children shouldn't be about their gender, but about the kind of adults we hope that they will be. We should provide a foundation for a fulfilling life where they are confident enough to be whoever they are and adapt to whatever life throws at them. It's not about teaching them to fit into prescribed moulds that are not actually useful or helpful in the long run.

That early education Mum gave me in the kitchen prepared me for a scenario that I would have never seen coming – me parenting solo while the mother of my child was seriously ill in hospital. It was stressful enough being worried about Candice, but if I hadn't had those basic, practical skills, that would have added a whole other level of stress. And yet, there are still some people who believe – even today – that a man's place is far from the kitchen and that there are certain roles only women should take on. Thankfully, Mum's education gave me the opportunity to view things differently. It gave me a different perspective than the typical patriarchal way of thinking. I can hand on heart say that if not for Mum's influence, I would have viewed my girls as different from my son – dare I say it? – even less than.

There are those who would say that gender roles are not that deep, since we have equality in more or less every other area of life. There was a time when – and there are still countries where – women could not buy a house by themselves, and they wouldn't be able to work outside of their home without their husband's permission. Compared to that, we've made leaps and bounds, so surely who cooks or cleans in our private homes is not that important? But we always have to ask ourselves the question: why do gender roles exist? Who ultimately benefits when we don't let children be children?

How do the limitations that we place on children inside the home affect the way they think about themselves, others, and what they can and cannot do outside of it?

The assumptions that we make about children based on their gender show us that we don't view children as individuals. Everyone is different, nobody is the same, and if there is one thing I have learned on my journey as a father, it is that children will teach you how to raise them. All you have to do is listen. They are often telling us what they want and how they want to be treated with every sound, tone, word, and their body language.

Children are products of their environments, and they watch everything we do. This is why Candice and I ensure that our kids do not feel limited because of their gender. RJ plays with dolls and a Hoover, and Esmé is madly in love with Formula 1, can name pretty much every car brand you can think of, and has even shown an interest in go-karting. I am all for the deconstruction of societal norms, especially around children and gender.

I often find myself asking who gets to set the measure of normal? Why is it difficult to find boys' clothing in pink? Why are there pink/unicorn toothbrushes for girls and blue/space toothbrushes for boys? Can't girls like space? Can't boys like unicorns?

Finding out the gender of my kids before they were born wasn't really a big deal for me. Whether we were having a boy or a girl, I just wanted a healthy baby. Even as Renae and Esmé have gotten older, I haven't felt the concerns that I know some men have about parenting girls. Some men worry about relating to their daughters and understanding what they're going through, which is fair enough, but because of my close relationship with my mum I've never had that concern. When Renae started her period, she was at our house, and she didn't tell me right away; she called her mum instead. Both Renae's mum and Candice have told me that there are just some things women have to deal with – but I can learn! I really believe there should be no conversation with any of my children that I cannot have. But, at the same time, I try to respect their boundaries when they draw them.

Speaking of conversations and boundaries, sex is an important one. Due to my kids' ages at the time of writing, we're in the early stages of this conversation. Though Esmé is a bright girl, I've only really started having in-depth conversations about this with Renae. It can be awkward at times but, again, it's about equipping her with the information she needs to make the right decisions for herself. It's about leaving the door open so she feels she can always talk to either of her parents comfortably about sex and relationships. Let's face facts: the children of this day and age are far more exposed then we were. For example, they have the internet where they can find pretty much anything. But still, I feel it is important for them to learn about these kinds of things from us, their parents, rather than some friend or the internet.

After having two daughters, I thought having a son wouldn't be that different, but as RJ has grown and as I consider how the world is set up, I know different conversations will need to be had. This is because of what society tells men versus what it tells women, which of course, I understand first hand. More than anything,

ALL YOU HAVE TO DO IS LISTEN

I need RJ to understand that men and women are equal. I need him to understand that he has no choice but to respect women, Black women most especially. I need him to understand that his gender gives him no superiority whatsoever and I also need him to understand that when women are talking about their experiences, it is not a time for him to share his opinions – it is a time for him to shut up and listen. Finally, I need him to understand that it is his responsibility to challenge his male friends any time they do anything to disrespect others. These are all things I wish I had learned earlier but, of course, most important for me is leading by example.

I cannot speak about this and not touch on the tense conversations I have had to have with family members, school, and other care settings when it comes to gendered expectations.

Here's another story for you. There was a time I sent RJ to nursery with pink pull-ups. I was asked by a member of staff to change them to blue. I was not surprised at this request because I knew exactly where it was coming from, but the truth is, when I was buying the pull-ups, I didn't pay attention to the picture on the pack. They were the exact same pull-ups, from the exact same brand, however one pack had blue pull-ups with a picture of a boy, and the other had pink pull-ups and a picture of a girl. I did not discover what I had done until I got home, but I just shrugged it off and said, 'Well, it's the same pull-up, isn't it?'

I also shrugged when the member of staff made her comment, but when we got home that evening, RJ refused to allow me to put the pink pull-ups on him.

When I asked him why, he said, 'Because it is for girls.' The next day, I raised this with the preschool, expressing my disappointment in their move to uphold gender stereotypes.

Why on earth would someone make a little boy feel he cannot wear pink pull-ups? There was no answer to my question. Instead, what I was met with was silence and someone who was clearly embarrassed. However, I could see that the message had been delivered how I'd intended. I could see that the cogs were turning and then I got an apology, which I refused to accept because an apology was not what I wanted. All I wanted to do was challenge a certain thought process.

I have also had the odd comment from family members about teaching Esmé and Renae how to clean the house because 'they are girls and they need to learn how to do that.' When I ask, 'What about RJ?' they respond by saying there is no need for him to clean.

The most important part of parenting for me is the ability to equip my children to be the best version of themselves, and most importantly, to know who they really are. I want to reach the point where I have laid a good enough foundation for that, rather than raising children how others 'believe' they should be raised according to their gender.

I would encourage each of us to spend time considering who our children are now. What do they like and not like? What are their hopes and aspirations? And how can we support them in growing confident of themselves and their convictions so, when others try to push them into boxes, they can boldly say what they do and do not want?

Modern parenting is hard with all the time pressures and distractions, but it's important for us to make time to really get to know our children as individuals. This can be done by encouraging more conversation around the dinner table, asking them questions about the things that interest them, as well as getting on our hands and knees and actually playing with them and their toys. Screen time is ever present, but instead of leaving them to their own devices, while we stay glued to ours, we can do things together on the tablet or computer — things that they enjoy and we can take part in.

Finally, I would encourage each of us to think about the things we wish we knew in our childhood, things we wish we'd been better prepared for, and also what character traits do we want our children to have. Thanks to social media, there are so many resources that can help and encourage us to build up traits such as empathy, resilience, self-control, and problem-solving in our kids. These are character traits that can be modelled or practised in the home, and they are important for every gender.

FATHERHOOD IN ACTION

So I say all of the above to ask you this:

What are you currently doing in your home and with your children to challenge gender stereotypes?

If you have a male child, what are you doing to ensure they grow up understanding their privilege as well as having respect for the opposite sex?

What are you doing to ensure that the voice of your female child is heard?

Did you know that cooking a simple recipe together with your children can be an exercise in problem-solving, as well as an important life skill? Teaching children to clean up after themselves also builds their independence and sense of responsibility. A study from the University of Minnesota even revealed that children who began doing simple chores around the house from as young as three or four went on to be more successful professionally, socially, and academically.[16] The idea that any of these skills should be restricted to a certain gender is ridiculous. Why not find a simple recipe you can cook with your child?

CHAPTER 7

DISCIPLINE

"Where did we ever get the crazy idea that in order to make children do better, first, we have to make them feel worse? Think of the last time you felt humiliated or treated unfairly. Did you feel like cooperating or doing better?"

– Jane Nelsen

I have seen, heard, and been involved in several discussions on the topic of discipline, and I have to say that within the Black community – specifically the Black African community, which I am part of – disciplining children involves the idea, 'spare the rod, spoil the child'. Remember I mentioned this earlier on? I am a product of such an environment and I know first-hand what it feels like.

Do I believe in physically disciplining children? The answer is a big NO – no ifs, buts, or maybes. I have my reasons for my views on this, and I feel I need to add here that this is based on my own experience. In several chapters of this book, I talk boldly about my relationship with my dad, and this includes his methods of raising children, specifically raising me, his first and only son.

The patriarchy has a lot to do with the ideas of what it means to raise boys who then go on to be men, fathers, and so on and so forth. As a parent, I have come to understand that it is one of my duties to guide my children on how to behave. This takes time and patience – a lot of patience, in fact. Put it this way, your children are sponges who learn from you by soaking up their environment, and if your answer to most things is a smack or another form of physical discipline – which, let's face it, comes from a place of anger – you are showing your children that the only way to deal with conflict is violence.

Do you see the problem here?

To fully understand this, especially when you are a Black person, you first of all need to reckon with the fact that slavery left a legacy of corporal punishment.

Dr Stacey Patton is an American author, journalist, and child advocate who established *Spare The Kids*!, a website dedicated to educating about the harm of corporal punishment and advising on gentler alternatives. In an essay she wrote for the American Psychological Association, she writes: 'A 2015 Pew Research survey found that Black parents are more than twice as likely as white and Latino parents to use corporal punishment on a regular basis, and they are far less likely to never spank their children. But while hitting children is prevalent in black communities, contrary to popular belief, it is not an intrinsic cultural tradition. Black parents have legitimate fears about the safety of their children, and the overwhelming majority believe physical discipline is necessary to keep black children out of the streets, out of prison, or out of police officers' sight. And far too many parents argue that "whupping" children is a distinctly black tradition. This belief, however heartfelt, is wrong.'[17]

Dr Patton goes on to explain how, in America, this acceptance of physical punishment is tied to the fact that Black children are more likely to be assaulted, seriously injured, or killed by a family member than by the police or a neighbourhood watchman. There also isn't any scientific evidence that beating your children will stop them 'turning out bad', especially in a society where unfortunately, due to systematic racism and bias, outcomes for Black children across the board tend to be worse than for white children.

I was having a conversation with Dad recently, which has become a bit of a norm in recent years, as I try to unpick a lot of his past behaviours, which somehow aids me on my journey of self-discovery. This conversation centred on physical discipline and of course he supports the idea, so much so, he told me that he felt I needed to do that a bit more with RJ, especially because 'he is a boy child'. Those were his exact words. This made me ask a lot of questions, the first being, 'What does being a boy have to do with it? Why him and not Esmé or Renae?'

His response was, 'You need to bring him in line and in check. He needs to understand his boundaries, especially in the country you live in. If you don't curb it now, it will become a serious issue for you in the future. If he does not learn to obey authority, it will be because he was not taught to do that from young.' I responded by asking why obedience has to come with physical discipline? I feel the moment an adult raises his or her hand to hit a child for whatever reason, is the moment all lessons said adult is trying to teach are lost. At that point you are basically telling the child, 'If you do this, you will get hit,' in addition to the fact that you are also telling the child that the best way to resolve conflict is with the fist.

The lesson you are trying to teach them gets lost because the child's focus is no longer on the act you are trying to correct but the physical pain you have caused

THERE IS A THIN LINE
BETWEEN RESPECT AND
FEAR, AND I FEEL THIS LINE
IS CROSSED VERY OFTEN.
I DO NOT WANT MY CHILDREN
FEARING ME. I WOULD LOVE
THEM TO RESPECT ME, BUT
THAT WILL ONLY HAPPEN IF
I AM WORTHY OF RESPECT.

with your hands. To quote a study conducted by the American Psychological Association, 'The research finds that hitting children does not teach them about responsibility, conscience development, and self-control. "Hitting children does not teach them right from wrong," says Elizabeth Gershoff, PhD, an expert on the effects of corporal punishment on children, who provided research for the resolution. "Spanking gets their attention, but they have not internalised why they should do the right thing in the future. They may behave when the adult is there but do whatever they want at other times.'[18]

I went on to tell my dad that there is a thin line between respect and fear, and I feel this line is crossed very often. I do not want my children fearing me. I would love them to respect me, but that will only happen if I am worthy of respect. I feel this way because I draw from my own lived experiences. I explained to Dad that my goal while growing up was to do things I knew he didn't like and not get found out. Honestly, there was a point when I actually didn't care about the physical pain from the smacking any more. After all, all I would get is a smack, right? I had trained my mind and body to accept it, deal with it, and move on.

So I asked Dad to tell me about the discipline methods used by his father. Surprisingly, my grandfather did not subscribe to physical discipline, in fact he never ever raised his hands. Dad told me a story. In the late seventies, early eighties, when Dad was preparing to travel to the UK for his university education, a leaving do was organised for him. Grandad got wind of the party and tricked Dad into paying him a quick visit under the guise of wanting to see what his travelling visa looked like. Upon arrival at Grandpa's house (at the time Dad lived with his cousins in Lagos), Grandpa seized the passport, which made Dad miss his flight. He was not able to travel until the following month. When Grandpa explained his reasoning to Dad, Dad fully understood. This shows the lesson was learned, if you ask me.

But what was Grandpa's message, I hear you ask?

Grandpa felt Dad had nothing to celebrate yet. Most of Dad's mates were already in university and some had already graduated, and it was these same friends that had put the party together. Grandpa told Dad it was absurd that *he* was celebrating as if he had already graduated from university. This was when he quoted a line that Dad went on to use over and over again in later years, and up until now when he gives advice to younger ones. The line was this: 'My friend is Zik [Nnamdi Benjamin "Zik" Azikiwe served as the first President of Nigeria from 1963–1966 and is known as the "father of Nigerian nationalism"], my friend is Awolowo [Chief Obafemi Jeremiah Oyeniyi Awolowo, a Nigerian nationalist and statesman who played a key role in Nigeria's independence movement, the First and Second Republics, and the Civil War] – who am I?' This basically means, be yourself and do not run on someone else's clock, dime, or reputation.

The way Grandpa used this line to teach my Dad is an approach I wholeheartedly believe in. This approach provides an explanation for the action taken by the parent, but it also creates an opportunity for the child to think, reflect, and come up with their own answers.

136

How many times have I heard the phrase, 'I do not have to explain my actions to my child'? As if the child lacks the ability to think or understand. Once the reasons for your actions are clearly explained to and understood by a child, it creates greater room for the learning of the lesson.

I found the story about Grandpa rather interesting because Dad most certainly did not parent or discipline like him, so where on earth did Dad get his ideas from? I found myself asking this out loud during the same conversation. He smiled and told me the story of his uncle in Lagos. Remember, I mentioned that my dad lived at his cousin's house? Well, this is where the story got interesting. Dad's uncle was a harsh disciplinarian often referred to as *Baba Leko* (Daddy in Lagos). He was a no-nonsense, hard-hitting kind of guy – the type who will make you run away when he approaches or returns home from work. It was quite apparent, from what Dad told me, that his uncle had a pretty rough upbringing and felt it was his duty to pass the suffering on, so to speak. He felt that the only way one can grow up from a child to a functioning member of society was through struggles and harsh discipline, which most certainly included a hell of a lot of physical beating.

Now here is the satisfying bit: after Dad told me the stories of his dad and uncle, I thought about the story of his uncle. I asked Dad if he understood what was going on there – the issue of transgenerational trauma and why it was important to break the cycle. I made the bold claim that Dad parented me solely out of fear. Not fear that I might not make something of myself, but fear of me turning out like him – meaning he was scared

BREAK
THE
CYCLE

that I would make the same mistakes he did. This was clearly not my cross to bear but his. However, because of his inability to deal with and process what was occurring, he simply passed the trauma on. This was a lightbulb moment and it was great to see Dad connect the dots during our conversation because he came to understand the reasons behind my choice to essentially chuck physical discipline out of my parenting toolkit.

When I said before that physical punishment is not necessarily intrinsic to culture in Black communities, I know some of you reading will disagree. But we really need to understand the history of corporal punishment and how it came to be embedded in our communities.

To put it simply: Black people, both those enslaved in America and the Caribbean and those living under colonial rule in their home countries, were influenced to beat their children by the white people who ruled over them. According to scholars and researchers, there is no evidence to show that, prior to slavery or colonialism, African people physically disciplined their children.

Going back to Dr Patton's essay for the American Psychological Association, she goes on to write that, 'West African societies held children in a much higher regard than slave societies in the Atlantic world, which placed emphasis on Black bodies as property, not as human beings. West Africans believed that children came from the afterlife, that they were gods or reincarnated ancestors who led profoundly spiritual lives and held extraordinary mystical powers that could be harnessed through ritual practice for the good of the community. In fact, it was believed that coercion and hitting a child could scare off their soul.'[17]

This rings true of conversations I've had with older members of my family. I was often referred to as the reincarnation of my grandfather, Dad's father. I was actually named after him, making my initials OBA (the direct translation of which, in English, is 'king') so it is no surprise to learn of his temperament with his children and the similarities we share. My auntie, Dad's immediate elder sister, once sat me down to explain the responsibility I had to carry because I was basically her father. She often called me *Baba mi* (my father), and she had various arguments with Dad regarding his disciplinary methods. She even once threatened to take me with her to the US, where she lived with her family.

In one of the many arguments they had in my presence, I heard her say that his idea of resorting to physical punishment was in fact creating opposite results to what he was trying to achieve. She said, 'Can you not see how it is making him retreat and enter his shell? This boy will grow up fearing everything and everyone!'

A study from the University of Ibadan in Nigeria on rural Yoruba communities acknowledges that while corporal punishment, or 'flogging', is indeed now widespread, Yoruba people have a number of different cultural ways of disciplining children and instilling the values that the community believes are important for an *iwa omoluabi* (good character). These methods include teaching through songs, proverbs, public correction, or warning, and even *oruko pipe* (name calling), which, considering the weight that is given by Yoruba people to the naming of their children, is no small thing.[19] But, as Dr Patton writes in her essay, 'As colonization, slavery and genocidal violence made life harsher for these groups, parenting practices also grew harsher.'[17]

But where did white people learn to beat their children? The influence is quite clear when you look at the Old Testament. *Proverbs* 29:15 reads, 'The rod and rebuke give wisdom, but a child left to himself brings shame to his mother.' The famous phrase, 'spare the rod, spoil the child,' comes from *Proverbs* 13:24: 'He who spares his rod hates his son, but he who loves him disciplines him promptly.'

In an article for Fatherly.com, writer Lauren Steele writes, 'As Puritans rose against the English church, the subjugation of children was formalised, dissuading them from challenging or rebelling against authority in the slightest. Puritan children were taught that by disobeying their parents they were forcing God to condemn them to eternal death, and that strong discipline i.e. physical punishment could bring salvation to children.'[20]

This is something I witnessed myself at school in Nigeria, bearing in mind the fact that I had a very British education at King's College, Lagos. I have vivid memories of public floggings during Friday or Monday assemblies for what was classed as 'bad behaviour' or behaviour that did not fit with what was classed as 'proper'.

As much as I disagree with the method of punishment, it is understandable that Black parents would resort to physical discipline when raising children in a world that has less tolerance for Black people who 'misbehave'. We all know what happened to George Floyd and how the narrative of him being a criminal remained an important part of the story – as if that somehow justified his treatment and murder by Derek Chauvin.[21]

Many adults live with the fear of police or government brutality and believe that forcing good behaviour on children when they are young could protect them from straying and ending up in worse trouble when they're older. Many of us have internalised the idea that the only way to keep our children safe is to get them to stay in line. And the only way to do that, is to beat them.

But a recent study published in *The Lancet* revealed that, while physical discipline may work in the short term, long term it actually makes children behave worse and be more aggressive, regardless of the culture, parenting style, race, or background of the children and parents involved.[22] Kellie Syfan, a behavioural analyst, told VerywellFamily.com that, 'Punishments increase avoidance behaviors, meaning that the person being punished will avoid the person who punishes them… and will do whatever they can to not get caught and avoid the punishment. This means that increases in lying and sneaking can occur.'[23] This is the point I always try to make in debates on the topic of discipline. I often say disciplining a child, especially when using − let's call it as it is − violence as the main tool, whether it is hitting or shouting (because violence isn't always physical), creates grounds for the lesson you are trying to teach to be missed. The message you are trying to teach gets lost as the child focuses on avoiding the violence, which will, in turn, lead to more bad behaviour.

Knowing and understanding all of the above is one thing, but taking active steps to change the narrative is another. I believe that once we gain knowledge on why things are a certain way, it should help us be able to decide on what steps to take next. My feelings on physical discipline come from understanding where I am from, where my parents and their parents are from, and what led to the decisions they took on a lot of issues.

I cannot explain it, but I know I made the decision to never physically discipline my children from a very young age because to me it felt wrong in so many ways. The idea of hitting someone that cannot hit back never sat right with me and I most certainly did not want my children to feel the same way I felt towards Dad whenever he raised his hand.

What we need to understand is, although children are young and may need guidance as they figure out who they are and who they want to become, they do have a mind of their own. We cannot force them to see things from our own perspective, even though this is exactly what physical discipline sets out to do. Physical discipline is to force our children to see things the way we see it, even though they don't – and never will – have the same experiences as us. So why would we think is it okay to force our thought processes on them?

Imagine trying to force your child to use an iPad the way you used your Nokia 3310 – it makes no sense, right? They now have *Subway Surf* on a device that is capable of doing all and more of what our parents' big-back Windows 95 computer on a painful dial-up internet system was capable of. It just does not work.

I also need to address the argument of 'different approaches' – where some people argue that certain children need a firmer hand. They make up reasons to defend or support physical discipline, like saying the

ALTHOUGH CHILDREN ARE YOUNG AND MAY NEED GUIDANCE AS THEY FIGURE OUT WHO THEY ARE AND WHO THEY WANT TO BECOME, THEY DO HAVE A MIND OF THEIR OWN.

THE MOMENT AN ADULT RESPONDS TO A CHILD'S 'MISBEHAVIOUR' WITH VIOLENCE, ALL LESSONS AND CONTROL ARE LOST.

child is too 'stubborn' or 'crafty'. To this I say, refer to earlier on in this chapter where I said that the moment an adult responds to a child's 'misbehaviour' with violence, all lessons and control are lost. It becomes your problem, not the child's. Let's face it, a child is unable to defend themselves against you, the adult, so I am sure you can see the lack of balance in this scenario.

Oftentimes behaviours and misbehaviours from children are a way of communicating; they are still developing these skills and lack a certain maturity that time and experience has taught an adult. They lack the ability to communicate in the way we as adults deem as proper. It is our duty, no matter how dire the situation is, to guide our children, not beat them because we feel a certain sense of dominion over them.

Another question that often arises is what happens when your child does something really wrong or bad? On this point we have to first realise that the measure of bad or wrong sits solely with us as adults. A young child is still learning and gaining experience and most certainly lacks the ability to understand right from wrong. You do not beat your dog when you are trying to teach it to sit. In a situation like this, I would resort to withholding an important toy while giving a very clear explanation for my action. This gives the child a way to fully understand that their action is the reason why they are no longer in possession of their toy. I try to ensure that I also leave space for repentance, for lack of a better word. This is when the child displays remorse and then I go over what is happening again, making sure the message gets delivered before handing back the toy.

I also get a lot of questions about the terrible twos, or toddler stages. Dr Jay L Hoecker, a doctor at the prestigious Mayo Clinic in Minnesota, USA, says, 'The term terrible twos has long been used to describe the changes that parents often observe in two-year-old children. A parent may perceive this age as "terrible" because of the rapid shifts in a child's mood and behaviors and the difficulty of dealing with them. One minute your child might be clinging to you, and the next he or she is running in the opposite direction.'[24]

However hard we find this point in our children's development, it's completely natural, but it does mean that us parents need to be patient with our kids and ourselves. Beating a two-year-old teaches them nothing – all it shows is that we've lost control of ourselves and the situation.

RJ is three and I distinctly remember him at toddler stage. He has constantly pushed boundaries and he still does. He is very strong-willed and knows what he wants and how he wants it, even though he is still pretty young. I remember a time he absolutely broke down in a public setting and I am sure anyone who is a parent has gone through this. It was so embarrassing; all eyes were on us. The little lad has some lungs on him, and I was so close to losing it, but I really had to have a conversation with myself in that very moment about how I was feeling. I mean, he was only two, and I only felt the way I was feeling because of other people, other people's eyes on us. I felt like we were being judged, but this helped me put things in perspective really quickly. He is my son, after all. What do other people's feelings have to do with it? I chose to comfort him in that moment. I carried him and gave him the biggest hug, and guess what? After five minutes he was asleep. Then I realised that he was tired and did not know how to communicate that, hence the breakdown.

FATHERHOOD IN ACTION

Flipping the script when it comes to discipline can be daunting, especially when it's all you've ever known. Maybe you've never seen other forms of discipline modelled successfully, but it is possible. Here are a few ideas and examples I have taken to change the narrative in my journey as a father and parent.

Offer a choice

I believe that offering children the opportunity to make choices and 'have a say' encourages them to have their own mind – and empowers them to make their own decisions. These skills come in handy when peer pressure starts to rear its ugly head. When you're regularly barking and shouting down at your children, ordering them around, constantly telling them to shut up and do what they are told, think about what might happen when someone else comes along that can shout just as loud as you and you are not around.

Choice is an act of choosing between two or more possibilities. This is often overlooked when bringing up children because we as adults feel they as children are unable to make the 'right' choices – ones that fit our standards. I will give you an example. Imagine your child comes to you asking for ice cream at 2 pm, when the usual time for ice cream is 6 pm, as dessert after dinner. In situations like this, as a parent you may be forced to say no immediately without any explanation, and this is because we may be programmed to offer no explanation to our children simply because we believe they have to listen to us. I would suggest a different approach here: instead of a flat-out no, how about we try something along the lines of, '[Child's name], you know we have ice cream after supper, so I need you to understand this: if you have the ice cream now, there will be none for you later when we are all having ours. Do you still want it?' If the child says yes, then by all means give the child that ice cream.

There is a very high chance that after supper, when everyone else is sat ready to have dessert, the child will ask for theirs. At this point, you as a parent can now answer the child with a no, but don't stop there. You have to explain why by tying it up with the choice you gave earlier. 'Remember you chose to have your ice cream at 2 pm? You were given the choice to wait for dessert or have it then and you chose to have yours earlier. You are going to have to accept that there is a consequence for every action.'

Of course, you may experience tears or tantrums at that point, but I promise you the lesson will have been learned, and I guarantee that next time (or in some cases, a few more times after that), the child will learn.

Flip the script

I think there is a growing trend around what some would call 'gentle parenting'. There are social media pages forming around communities of parents who are interested in this different approach, and they share tips and expert advice. These pages could be a good place to start as you begin on this journey because, whether you find that community online or in person, you don't have to do this thing alone.

I am sure by now you have come to understand that I am all about challenging the norms, and how I do this is by deconstructing and reconstructing. You just have to ask yourself one question: if you hated it as a child, what makes you think your child wouldn't hate it too? You hated it because it was not right, so why not take active steps to change it?

CHAPTER 8

FINANCIAL RESPONSIBILITY

"A formal education will make you a living; self-education will make you a fortune."

– Jim Rohn

'What do you want me to do? Quit my job and stay home to look after the baby with you while I claim benefits, further increasing our financial issues?'

This was a question I once asked Candice during a big argument about the amount of time I was not spending at home.

As I've said, Nigeria, the country I spent my formative years in, was and still is hugely patriarchal. There, the belief is that the man is the head of the household. The role of a man is to provide financially – nothing is more important than that. And a woman? In Nigeria, the general belief is that the best place for a woman is in the kitchen.

Here is where we need to talk about gender.

Gender refers to the socially and culturally constructed roles for men and women. For instance, the role of men as owners of property, decision makers, and heads of household are historically, culturally, and socially constructed ideas that have nothing to do with biological differences.

I have often listened to female friends in Nigeria complain about how they are treated when purchasing goods and services. For example, when looking for a place to live, whether it be rental or purchase, they are often asked by the landlord or seller of their marital status. If they respond by saying they're single, they often end up losing said property unless they can provide details of a male sponsor to stand in as guarantor. How galling! Can you imagine needing the presence of a man to justify your worth, or your existence?

A single, successful woman in Nigeria is often not respected in the same way a man would be. You only need to venture onto Nigerian Twitter to see complete strangers responding to a woman tweeting her success with comments such as, 'What's a successful woman without a man?' or debates on whether a woman should ever earn more than her husband.

I will take this back to my parental family set up: as expected, Dad was the sole breadwinner. I was told a story by Mum about how she was coerced into giving up an amazing job as the head librarian at a major print media company, which was owned by Dad's family. Mum was pressured by my dad into becoming a stay-at-home-wife, or 'housewife', as she often called herself. She hated the idea of that but had no choice because this was the way. After all, who was going to look after the home, the children, and her husband while she was at work?

After that, Mum became financially dependent on Dad for everything, even for money to purchase sanitary items, and I know for a fact that Mum hated all of this, especially when he questioned the cost of items she put on the shopping list.

This was primarily the reason why I decided when I was young that if I was ever to get married or be in a relationship, it had to be with a person who was unlike

Mum. This is not because Mum is not an amazing person – she is truly one of a kind, and I need to make that very clear. It is just that I saw first-hand what all of this did to her, and for that very reason I wanted to be with someone who had her own.

Now, I feel I need to clarify a few things: my yearning for someone who had hers was not because I didn't want to provide; in so many ways I am pretty old fashioned, so to speak. I dreamed of being in a position where I would be able to provide, but not in the position where the person I was with relied on me for everything. Not to the point where she could not breathe without me. I felt this was quite counterproductive and a lot of pressure for me.

Even though, generally, there has been progress on many fronts with gender equality – which is a human right – we are so far from where we need to be. The UN says, 'Despite progress, women and girls around the world do not fully experience equal rights and their potential as economic, social, and sustainable development change-agents remains untapped. Women are underrepresented in power and decision-making roles. They receive unequal pay for equal work and they continue to be targets of physical and sexual abuse. Additionally, women-owned enterprises are economically disadvantaged and lack equal opportunity to compete for business opportunities. Women also face legal and other barriers that affect their opportunities at work and as entrepreneurs.'[25]

Now, back to the beginning of this chapter. The burden of financial responsibility rested heavily on my shoulders, not because anyone put it there, but because

MY VALUE AS A MAN WAS BASED ON WHAT I DID FOR WORK

of societal pressures. I grew up in a household where the man – my father – was the sole provider. This was also the case with a lot of the men in his friendship groups. They were men who were proud of who they were, and they commanded a lot of respect for the roles they played in their various households. Whenever we visited Dad's friends, mostly on weekends, the men would gather in the living room while the women stayed in 'their space'… the kitchen.

Mum ran a few businesses of her own, set up for her by Dad, but this did not change anything. Remember, he was the king of his castle – the buck stopped with him. As a male, I was taught from a young age that my sole purpose was to provide financially for my family. If, for some reason, I were to find myself in a situation where I was unable to do that, I would automatically become a failure and less of a man. I was taught that nothing else mattered. I had no business cooking, I had no business washing dishes, I had no business cleaning the house, I had no business engaging in any domestic activities, I had no business sitting down at home to look after the kids. All I had to do was go to work, earn a living, and provide.

All of this made the thought of doing anything else apart from providing seem pretty unattractive to me. I mean, when Esmé was born, I was working damn hard for a salary of approximately £23,000 a year (before tax). I was doing my best to put food on the table but anything outside of that was something I, and we, simply could not afford. When things grew tense between us, I often thought to myself, 'Can Candice not see how hard I am trying? Can she not see that I am working so damn hard to provide, that I'm not spending any of this money on myself? What else does she want me to do?'

I remember having this conversation with a very close friend after a big argument with Candice, an argument so big that I was almost sure we were over as a couple. My friend listened to me ramble on for a long time without saying a word. When I was done, he asked me two simple questions: 'Have you stopped for a second to listen to her without thinking about your masculinity?' and 'Why do you feel so threatened?' The questions made me go quiet for a while. I was piecing it all together. I was becoming that very thing I swore I wouldn't be. I was becoming that guy. I was feeding into the narrative of the patriarchy.

I asked myself these questions:

What did I think my contribution was? And what did I think it was meant to be?

What was I placing value on? Was it on the same things Candice classed as important?

This is an example of why communication is very important in any relationship. I have now come to understand – they do say hindsight is a beautiful thing – that I was placing all the value on money, as if money was the single most important thing in our relationship and lives. I felt my value as a man was based on what I did for work, what I got paid from that work, and how I was able to financially look after everybody. The moment I became unable to do that, for whatever reason, I would become less than, and I would no longer deserve the title of 'man'.

Does this sound familiar? I have spoken to a lot of men, old and young, and we always arrive at the same conclusion. Candice, on the other hand, placed all value on time spent with family. The only contribution of mine that she was judging was how much time I spent, physically and emotionally, doing my part as a father to our child. Was I there for breakfast? Was I there to put her to sleep? Was I there to spend time with her in the park? Most importantly, was I there to support where it was required the most?

I had to do a lot of work on myself to shake the belief that one's value is equal to one's job and earnings. The part of the world I come from places a lot of emphasis on this. As a boy, the importance of having a career and money was drummed into me, hence why Dad never liked it when Mum dragged me into the kitchen and not my sisters. In his eyes, the kitchen was no place for a man — it was my sisters' duty to learn how to look after their husbands by feeding them, cleaning after them, and taking care of the children. It would be my job to provide financially — and this was non-negotiable.

I began to realise that, just like I had decided to question other ideologies instilled in me from my younger years, my thoughts about financial responsibility in the household needed questioning and deconstructing. I had grown to see Mum's reliance on Dad for anything financial. It took a lot out of her to go, as an adult and a grandmother, to another adult — albeit her husband — to ask for money to get her hair done, for example, only to be met with questions about the cost of what she wanted to get done. That, in my opinion, was degrading and definitely something I was not prepared to subscribe to. I did not have to stick to old blueprints.

I had to decide what was important for my family and for me, as a man, partner, and father.

I have come to understand that the idea of 'Financial Responsibility' is quite dynamic, which was a massive revelation for me. For a while, I was the breadwinner, which gave Candice the ability to really work on her craft. This created some room for change, which then meant we had to recalibrate and re-evaluate. There is no way our relationship would have been as successful as it is if I was still stuck in my old way of thinking, the way I was taught to think by society.

That was a turning point for us.

A few years later, Candice's career really started to take off and our union had become more like a partnership. I would go out to work, earning a steady income (which had increased exponentially by this time), and she would continue to build her career. After a while, Candice started to out-earn me by a lot and, contrary to how I was raised, I was really happy about this.

Once the idea of how one adds value shifts, you start to understand that it is more of a team effort – and that society's idea of who should do what within a household is pretty skewed. Because of the change in perspective, I was comfortable that Candice was earning more than me. The value I added was not trying to compete with her by chasing a bigger pay cheque, but it was by being around more, and being more supportive, physically and emotionally.

By this point, I was becoming pretty bored with my chosen career as a business development director. I had no interest in it anymore and I wanted to do something for me, to chase my dreams so to speak. This was most

RESPONSIBILITY IS NOT ALL ABOUT HOW WELL A MAN PROVIDES IN TERMS OF MONEY, BUT HIS CONTRIBUTION TO THE UPLIFTMENT OF THE FAMILY.

certainly inspired by Candice and how she went after what she wanted, and achieved it. She made me realise there is more to life. The truth is, as a man with children, chasing one's dreams becomes a bit of a risky gamble that can be quite costly, but here I was, looking for something better and also safe in the knowledge that I had the security to do this.

So here are my thoughts on this topic. Let us ditch the old-school idea of a man's value being tied to his money or career, and of a woman's value to how good she is at cooking or looking after the kids. Responsibility is not all about how well a man provides in terms of money, but his contribution to the upliftment of the family.

FATHERHOOD IN ACTION

To really change how we think, we need to question and examine our personal ideas about value. Talking about values is a touchy subject because it often goes down to the core of our being. It affects what we believe about ourselves and others. So maybe the best place to start addressing this issue is with ourselves.

Take a quiet moment to think and reflect on the following questions:

What have I been taught to value in myself?

What have I been taught to value in a parenting partner?

Think about the messages you learned by example from the adults or guardians of your childhood, and also the messages you received as you have grown. These can be anything, from the way one parent spoke about another parent, to the things you have been complimented on or criticised about as a parent yourself.

I recommend you write this all down in a journal or notebook. Then go through all those messages and think about which values you want to hold on to, and which should be let go. Add any other values you may have picked up along the way that you think are important.

Then, from that list, identify which three are most important to you, tell yourself why they are important, and think about what it means to honour those values in your life on a day-to-day basis.

This could be an exercise that both you and your partner do separately, before you come together to talk about it. You might want to discuss the values that were impressed upon you as a child and how they have been helpful or unhelpful, or you could skip ahead to speak about the top three values each of you has identified.

In all likelihood, you are going to have two different lists. So how can you negotiate with each other's concerns so you can work better as a team? If one of you values physical presence and quality time over financial provision, what can you do to meet in the middle and ensure that not only are the material needs for your family met, but that everyone feels valued in their contribution?

Sometimes it can be as simple as verbal recognition: 'I see how hard you work and, while I do wish you were around more and able to attend the kids' Christmas play with me, I'm grateful that you are doing your best to ensure that our expenses are covered each month.'

These kinds of conversations are never easy, and if you aren't used to communicating on these types of topics, you are probably going to put your foot in your mouth at some point, but it's an important conversation to have. And with patience you can get there. Remember, when it comes to your family life, you and your partner are on the same team. Sometimes you're just expressing your support in different languages.

CHAPTER 9

WORK-LIFE BALANCE

"The division of one's time and focus between working and family or leisure activities."

– Oxford English Dictionary

The act of balancing my work life and home life was an absolute struggle, and it caused a lot of arguments that did not need to happen. I come from an environment where, as a man, it is absolutely rammed into you that you need to work hard to provide for your family, and that alone is your duty. Do not get me wrong, I still believe in the idea of working hard in life to achieve what you want; the difference is, now I know that hard work only gets you a fraction of what you desire. Working hard and expecting that to be the answer to everything is like driving your car without knowing how to get to your desired destination.

According to Mentalhealth.org, 'The pressure of an increasingly demanding work culture in the UK is perhaps the biggest and most pressing challenge to the mental health of the general population.

The cumulative effect of increased working hours is having an important effect on the lifestyle of a huge number of people, which is likely to prove damaging to their mental well-being. The Mental Health Foundation is concerned that a sizable group of people are neglecting the factors in their lives that make them resistant or resilient to mental health problems.

One in six of us will experience a mental health problem in any given week, and our mental health awareness day research this year suggests that a majority of Britons have experienced some kind of mental health problem, with young adults especially open about this when surveyed.

What's clear then is that in our workplaces and in our circles of friends, there are people living with mental health problems, or just keeping themselves afloat, whether we know it or not. Work-related stress already costs Britain 10.4 million working days per year.

The human costs of unmanaged work-related stress extend far beyond this. A key way to protect your mental health against the potential detrimental effects of work-related stress is to ensure you have a healthy work-life balance.'[26]

I find the above statement rather fascinating, considering that the idea of giving your all at work, and making yourself available at any given time, is still the order of the day in most businesses – most certainly in almost all the businesses I have worked for. Reading that really helped me understand and come to terms with the fact that I too was suffering from work-related stress, and I therefore decided to do something about it.

I think I need to add a disclaimer here: I am in no way suggesting anyone should quit their job, or trying to say that working in a typical nine-to-five profession is wrong. But for me it just didn't work. I worked out early on that I am a creature of habit with quite an addictive personality. This is the reason I don't gamble and never have, and this is also the reason why I don't do drugs and never have. What I did do, though, was pour everything I had into work.

I had experienced Dad working so hard to provide and I wanted to ensure I was doing the same. I started working at the age of nineteen – while I was at university – to supplement the pocket money I got from Dad. I loved partying and going to nightclubs, so I needed some extra cash to fund my lifestyle. I worked in various retail jobs, including at a very well-known department store in the centre of London, which was a memorable one – and not for good reasons at all. I remember one time when my line manager told me to be careful with the way I handled the luxury merchandise because I would never be able to afford a single item. I must admit this was one of the things I held in my back pocket and used as fuel to keep working hard. (Side note: I visited the Tom Ford concession in the same department store a year ago to purchase a few items, and there he was serving me, the same line manager, almost seventeen years after my last day in the job. We shared a laugh and parted ways.)

After a few years in fashion retail, I decided I needed a bit of a change and got a job at the now defunct Phones 4u. It was around that time my relationship with Renae's mum broke down. The birth of Renae was a steep learning curve for me. The pressure was on. All of a sudden, there was this little girl that I was responsible for and I was really hard on myself because I felt I had wasted so much time before then partying and not planning for the future. I always felt I was not doing enough, and this showed in my behaviour and contributed to the toxicity seeping out of every pore of my body. I still loved the things I'd enjoyed doing before having a child, so I felt my freedom was being taken away from me – a freedom I felt I had only just gained after leaving the shores of Nigeria for my university. I resented it.

When I look back now, I realise I cannot quite put my finger on what I worked for, and why. I just worked so hard because this is what I believed to be the right and only way to be a man. As long as I held a job, I was a man. I was a man and a father, and nothing else.

In my early twenties, I found a job in the corporate world and I was determined from day one to make a career out of it. This was shortly after I came back from Nigeria where I had hit the reset button after my break-up with Renae's mum. I don't know what it was, but I had pep in my step. However, I was about to start out in an industry that I had no experience or knowledge of.

So there I was, starting out at a multi-million-pound company. And I had no idea how many hours I'd need to put in at my new job, or how little time I'd get to spend with my family.

Even now, Esmé still does not allow me to put her to bed. She always asks for her mum, and when her mum is not at home – if she is working away or returning later than bedtime – she sorts herself out. I know exactly why this is the case.

During her younger years, I was never around. I had worked hard enough to get into a senior management position that paid quite well, so life was indeed good: bills were paid, the fridge was full. But at home the damage was already done and we were almost at the point of no return. I spent so much time trying to impress my bosses, I spent so much time ensuring that I was at the forefront of everyone's mind anytime a position came up, that I didn't realise my family and my child needed me more.

Those early years of working on my career was taking its toll on my relationship with Candice. I would leave the house on Monday only to return on Friday because the job took me up and down the country. I was hardly ever at home. Candice had to look after Esmé by herself most of the time. This didn't bother me at the time because, in my mind, I was out there working to provide and, as far as I was concerned, there was no other way. I would get home on Friday, expecting to be welcomed with open arms like a soldier returning from battle to his loved ones, only to be met with hostility, which at the time felt totally unfair. I mean, I wasn't out there partying and acting a fool, I was actually out there slugging it out in a job that, let's be honest, I was no longer enjoying. But that was what I believed. In my mind, that was the only way to be a man and a father. Whenever Candice complained, I dismissed her by saying how unfair she was being, and asking her questions like, 'Do you want me to stay at home being a bum?'

One would think that I would make up for lost time on the weekends and evenings when I didn't have to work away, but sadly this was not the case. As I mentioned earlier, I was so committed to work that I found myself working on my laptop during those times, completing admin.

Things started to change ever so slightly the day Candice met me as I returned from work. She was holding Esmé. She literally didn't even wait for me to get out of the car, she handed Esmé to me through the lowered car window. As we walked to the house, she gave me an ultimatum, asking me to choose between her and Esmé, and my job. She also said something I'd never thought of. She said, 'Bodé, do you really think the company you work for will fight so hard to keep you if there was a cost-cutting exercise?' I, of course, responded by saying I was a valued member of staff and it was impossible for them to let go of me. This was when she said something so simple yet so powerful, it broke through my defences instantly. Sarcastically, she said, 'Oh yes, and if you die, the company will cease to exist.'

What a kicker that was. That statement really pissed me off. I started to shake immediately, and the level of anger in me at that moment could break the hardest bit of concrete you could think of. It knocked the wind out of me and I started to hyperventilate. Luckily Esmé was in a different room by this point. My body's reaction to what Candice had said was so visceral, I had to leave the room immediately. In fact, I picked up my car keys and drove away dramatically – the tyre marks are still on our driveway, where they serve as a constant reminder.

Something amazing happened on that drive, though. Like I always do, I started to self-analyse and ask myself questions. *Why did that statement cut so deep?* Was it because Candice was speaking the truth? She had seen right through my defences and cut through my bullshit. I had witnessed first-hand other employees that I would class as more valuable than me get cut without a moment's notice, so what made me think it could never happen to me? At the same time, one saying I'd heard a while back kept playing in my head: 'It is madness to keep doing the same thing over and over expecting different results.'

It was at that moment I realised I had missed so many milestones. I missed when Esmé took her first steps, I missed when Esmé uttered her first word – which was 'mama', no surprise there – I missed so many bedtimes I couldn't even remember bedtimes apart from the first month after her birth (when I was on paternity leave). My relationship with Candice was going in the wrong direction. We argued a lot and it felt as if we were growing apart super-fast. Then I thought about my job and how things were going, and I knew deep inside that I hated it. There was a lot of pressure, which made me really cranky most of the time. I came to the conclusion that the company I worked for lacked respect for its employees and their personal lives. It was the company's fault!

Yes, I came to that conclusion after all of that, after everything that Candice had pointed out. This was a conclusion that clearly showed a lack of taking responsibility, a conclusion that showed I didn't really understand what was happening. But I didn't see that, so I made the decision to join another business in the same industry, hoping things would change. After all, it was the company, not me, right?

I settled into the new job easily. I was happy and things seemed better at home. Once the third month came and the novelty of the new job wore off, I started to have that same feeling all over again – the feeling that something was missing. Candice and I started to

I REALISED THERE WAS MORE TO MANHOOD AND FATHERHOOD THAN THE ABILITY TO HOLD DOWN A JOB AND PROVIDE FINANCIALLY.

have arguments again, and while this company had a bit more respect for family time and there was less cross-country travel, which meant I returned home every day, I still had to leave the house at ungodly hours. By this time, we had moved to Milton Keynes and my office was based at Heathrow, which meant I never saw Esmé in the morning.

The truth was I felt empty. I started to have difficult conversations with myself once again, centred around the following points: yes, the work culture in the previous company was toxic and this one was most definitely not the same, but why did I still feel this way? I came up with more questions than answers.

It was around this time that we found out RJ was going to make an appearance, and I found myself wanting to play a bigger part than I had when Esmé was born. I realised there was more to manhood and fatherhood than the ability to hold down a job and provide financially. I started to really research the rules around paternity leave. I had a few conversations with some men that I call friends and they all felt the same way. Yes, you read that correctly: all of them felt that way. They all felt they were fighting a losing battle, they were all having arguments with their significant others and felt somewhat underappreciated, and they all said the whole situation was unfair – after all, all they were trying to do was provide.

I say all of them, but let me rephrase that, all of them except one. Let us refer to him as Jonathan. Jonathan wasn't fighting a losing battle: he had taken it a step further by resigning from a company where he was part of the board. In his words, he'd had enough of missing out on family time, especially with his kids, and he felt nothing was more important to him than being there with his kids, sharing those key moments. I felt like he was the bravest man on earth and I admired him, although I was not yet ready to take such a huge step.

But still, I felt I needed to make changes. I needed to make changes because I had gotten it all wrong. The first thing I did was request extended time off work to be there with Candice and Esmé when RJ was born. I took an amazing eight weeks off work. Of course, I was met with all the judgemental looks and questioning (as described in chapter 3). Someone was even bold enough to ask me if *I* was the person giving birth!

The decision was not taken lightly at all and I remember talking to Dad about it. He thought I was going crazy. He said something that was the final nail in the coffin for me – my epiphany, so to speak. He asked if the company I worked for was going to take me seriously and see a future with me after I requested extended time off to be with my family during and after the birth of my son. Let's face facts: many companies still see the women as the child rearers. Even today, many men experience a certain level of friction and disdain whenever there is mention of extended paternity leave. My dad asked how my clients were going to feel – if they would feel abandoned or left out. It was at that very moment I realised my priorities had been totally and utterly wrong. I had never put myself first during my career, I had always put the company's interests before anything else – before my family and, most importantly, before myself.

That was my turning point. During my time off on paternity leave, I started to lay down the plans for my exit strategy. The first thing was to put boundaries in place. Shortly after my return to work, I decided to leave the company and return to my old employer. Remember them, the multi-million-pound company I worked for in the past? Yes, that one. They had courted me ever since I'd left and I finally gave in. But before I accepted the offer to return, I stated my boundaries and rules of engagement. I said no phone calls from anyone – regardless of position held or monies spent – outside of working hours, and this most certainly included weekends. I would not be responding to emails outside of working hours, which most certainly included weekends. If anyone planned conference calls outside of working hours, they would need to count on the fact that I would not be attending. And lastly, I would not, for any reason, spend a single night out of my house, so if I had to attend any meetings away from London and the South East, they had to ensure it ended in good time for me to return home. For me, this was the beginning of boundary setting and the perfection of work-life balance.

During my time trying to figure things out, I decided that the idea of a 'work-life balance', in itself, is flawed. I found myself asking, why does 'work' come before 'life'? I figured out that it is this way because it seems as though the ultimate goal in life for most people is getting rich as quickly as possible so they can then travel the world, relax on a tropical island, or just live life without worrying about income. All of those aspirations are great! Who wouldn't want to do those things? And if that's what's going to bring the most joy into your life, you should WORK towards it! However, what dreams like these may do is create an environment where you cease to exist in the present, where you don't take note of what is most important or spend much-needed time with those you love the most.

In short, many of us dream of and work for a future that we have not yet experienced and, let's be honest, might not become a reality because it is life – anything can happen! What this does, is it stops us from fully immersing ourselves in the now. And ultimately, it is the now that dictates the future.

For the first few months back at the company, things were going well. My boundaries were being respected, though I wish I could say it continued. Sadly, it didn't. I started to notice a return to old ways with a few phone calls here and there. I remained strong and resolute. I did not answer any of the calls and responded to no emails that came outside of working hours, so much so that one day I had a one-to-one review scheduled with my line manager at a hotel in Heathrow. It was at 9 am on a Monday morning, and don't forget I live in Milton Keynes, which meant that in order for me to get to the venue in good time, I would have needed to leave my house at 6 am, which I did.

The first thing my line manager asked me at exactly 9:05 am was about the details of the weekly financial report that is normally sent every Sunday evening. My response to him was, 'I have no clue.' He went bright red with anger immediately, and proceeded to berate me for my lack of knowledge of the financial numbers. Right then I realised my time was up, I had to leave. The rest of our conversation was very uncomfortable because I chose to challenge him on what I classed as a very unreasonable question, especially since he knew

MANY OF US DREAM OF AND WORK FOR A FUTURE THAT WE HAVE NOT YET EXPERIENCED . . . WHAT THIS DOES, IS IT STOPS US FROM FULLY IMMERSING OURSELVES IN THE NOW.

full well what my boundaries were. I pointed out the fact that the numbers he was asking for were sent on a Sunday evening, which was clearly out of working hours, and considering the time of our meeting, there was no way I would have had time to open up said report. Let us just say that I ended up walking away from that meeting abruptly and handed in my resignation a few months later. I was not willing to sacrifice a minute of my personal time.

I must add, that my position at this moment was one of privilege: there was another wage coming in to the household, one that dwarfed what I was making from my job. In other words, I had a certain level of security, which gave me the option of quitting my job when I wanted to.

Being honest with myself about the job and my boundaries was glorifying, it was freeing. But I think a few things are worth discussing, for example, why didn't I want to just leave corporate life altogether? Why was it such a struggle?

This is something I have thought about quite a lot while reflecting, and I have come up with a few answers that fit the narrative, so to speak. For me, I saw no other way out. I felt this was the only way for me to provide and be there for my young family. I come from a place where your worth is measured by the work you do and how much you earn. This is also why there is such an emphasis on education. Dad wanted me to become an economist or lawyer. I feel it is important to add that he regrets not studying law himself. In Nigeria, you will find job adverts that don't just state that a degree is required, but that also dictate the grade required, which is typically in the region of a minimum second–class upper (2:1). In some cases, a university degree is not enough. You also need to show proof of further professional courses.

So leaving the corporate world just made no sense to me at all. Then, throw in my need and want to over-assess every situation before I take any step or make any move. I often describe Candice as the type to jump off a cliff without caring how she is going to land. For me, that would seem pretty strange, and Candice often gets frustrated with me over how long I take to make a decision. I am the type to assess all possible risks and outcomes; I need to know exactly where and how I am going to land, and what I need to do to ensure my landing is soft and smooth. Add to this an employer that takes everything you have to offer and makes you feel like you cannot succeed without them, plus the fact I was an immigrant in a country I had moved to in order to make something for myself – and you start to see how leaving my corporate job became a very scary prospect.

But I finally did take that step and leave the corporate world. This happened at the beginning of a global pandemic. I must say that being stuck behind a computer with nowhere to go, making a few phone calls to clients between 8 am and 5:30 pm every day while the kids were out in the garden begging for my attention, really made me start looking at things differently. I reflected a lot and realised I no longer wanted to be in that job. At that point, Candice was doing really well. Quite frankly, she was in a position to cover all necessary bills so I probably did have a bit of a soft landing after all.

IT WAS FREEING

One calm evening, Candice sat me down and asked the question I knew was coming. She led with a statement, which was, 'I know that look – you hate it.' I tried to pretend by putting on a smile while cracking a joke, but she was not letting go. Boy, she dug deeper and hit me with the question, 'How long are you going to continue like this for? How long are you going to continue pretending? How long are you going to be moany and sometimes irritable? When are you going to be bold enough to chase your dreams?' I had no answer for that. I knew deep down inside that she was right, and that was when she hit me with the sucker punch: 'Look, Bodé, you have been talking about starting your own business and doing the things you love. What happened to those dreams? Honestly, can you actually tell me what is stopping you from chasing those dreams right now? What is stopping you from leaving your job to focus on what you love?' I tried the old trick – answering with, 'Money. How do I pay bills?' but Candice looked at me with that 'Boy, don't take me for an idiot' look so I changed my answer to, 'Nothing. Nothing is stopping me. I can actually do it.' And that was pretty much it. I resigned the very next day.

As I write this, I look back now and think to myself, 'Gosh, why did I not do it sooner?' But I also understand that nothing happens before its time. I had to be ready. And I have to admit I am now having the time of my life. Over the years, I created a certain structure around myself, purely because I'd realised early on that I have an addictive personality. I felt unable to concentrate on more than one thing at a time, so it felt impossible to chase or build a career if I was distracted by things that made me feel more human. So I had no hobbies; I did nothing for myself.

The structure in my mind was so strict that it even became apparent in my physical appearance. In the past, I'd enjoyed the exploration of fashion and colour (so much so that a friend I attended university with – who is now a badass bespoke suit tailor – mentioned to me recently that he got his initial inspiration from me), but there I was, living a life that lacked any kind of colour – right down to my wardrobe! Candice often joked about my clothing. She would say, 'All you have in there is black, grey, and navy blue.' But thankfully, after a while focusing more on myself, I was back to living life in colour!

So, the other day I ticked something off my bucket list – I flew a damn plane! I shared the video of me flying the plane with my friends in our WhatsApp group, and one of them replied, 'Bodé Aboderin, you have started LIVING. Can you see the difference?' This friend was the first one in my group of friends to give up the corporate life in Nigeria, where he was pretty high up, to start a business he was really passionate about. I had watched him change, I'd watched him start to embrace and enjoy life and, most importantly, I'd watched his family life absolutely flourish.

In the space of a year, I have learned that there is more to life than chasing a job and job titles; I have learned that no achievement, accolade, or promotion at work can take the place of smiles on the faces of my kids – the smiles I see more often, now that I am able to spend more time with them building LEGO or Duplo, painting, drawing, doing silly stuff like dancing to the soundtrack of the *Trolls,* movie or just indulging in eating ice cream at midday. Most importantly, I feel I am more present in the life of all my children than I have ever been in their short lives – and I am here for all of this.

Now here are some important things: I am not telling anyone to leave their job in pursuit of a better life. I am fully aware that one size does not fit all – that different people have different set-ups and circumstances. However, there are some practical things we can all do a bit more to improve our work-life balance.

Establish boundaries – never underestimate the power of boundaries. Companies are there to take as much as possible from you as long as you are willing to give it, so start setting your boundaries, your non-negotiables. You have to figure out what is most important to you. In this day and age, where flexible working is becoming more acceptable, it is wise to take that opportunity and assess your working conditions. If the company you work for is not willing to accept your boundaries then I am afraid that company is not a good fit for you – not the other way round.

Play to your strengths – don't try to be all things to all people. You are not Superman, you are not superhuman, you are, in fact, human like everyone else, flaws and all.

Prioritise your time – ensure that you come first, followed by your family if you have one. It is important to note the order; you cannot pour from an empty cup. Understand that you must look after yourself first and foremost. Seems like a no brainer, right? Often, that is one of the hardest things to practise.

Know your peaks and troughs – this automatically reduces the risk of burnout, which is quite common in this day and age, when the workplace is demanding more than ever from its employees. Figuring this out helps you to decide when to say yes or no, and when you will have the brainpower to carry out requested tasks. What I mean is, no one is able to operate at optimum level all the time – you've got to know when and how to switch off at the appropriate time.

Plot some personal time – this, for me, is one of the most important things. Outside of your family and job, you are your own person. It is quite easy to muddle these things up, especially when you are chasing a career. I found this to be the case on my journey. I had no personal life or hobbies, so when it came down to it, I quickly realised I was nothing outside of my job.

Have set work hours (and, if you are self-employed, a set workspace) – if there is one thing you take away from this chapter, let it be this. This should be an absolute non-negotiable, and it ties in nicely with the establishment of boundaries.

Leave work at work – don't be a martyr. As someone who dealt with and continues to deal with the so-called 'saviour's complex', I know this all too well. The need to impress my bosses so I would be considered for the next promotion was a recipe for disaster, especially with a young family involved. I often found myself agreeing to take up tasks that I knew full well would add to time spent away from family. It was so unnecessary. I look at job ads nowadays and kiss my teeth when I spot the 'ability to go above and beyond' line. I know first-hand how destructive it is to employees, and I'm not saying this is the case at every company, but just think for a second: will the business go above and beyond for you?

FATHERHOOD IN ACTION

Here are a few questions you can ask yourself to find out whether your work-life balance needs an adjustment.

- How satisfied are you with your current work hours?

- How often do you work overtime?

- Could you benefit from offloading some of your tasks to another employee?

- Have you missed a personal event because of work?

- How satisfied are you with your current work-life balance?

- How often do you take work home?

- How often do you work on the weekend?

- How often do you work on vacation?

- Do you check emails after you leave the office?

- Are you satisfied with your work schedule?

- How many hours do you sleep on an average work night?

- How strongly do you agree or disagree with the following statements?

  - I prioritise my job over my personal life.

  - I prioritise my family over my work.

  - I sacrifice sleep to spend time with my family.

CHAPTER 10

THE POWER OF SPIRITUALITY, NETWORKS & SUPPORT GROUPS

"If you want to go somewhere, it is best to find someone who has already been there."

– Robert T Kiyosaki

I grew up in a Christian home, a very strict one, in fact. I distinctly remember prayer time every evening, and I disliked it so much that I found myself falling asleep almost every time, only to be woken up by Dad with a whack on the head as he shouted my name, or by the careful nudge of one of my sisters as they tried to help me hide the fact I was falling asleep, since they knew all hell would break loose. Religion was such a big deal back home in Nigeria, where the main religions are Christianity and Islam.

When I was younger, I would say I had no issue making and maintaining friendships. Without full awareness of the expectations that go along with my gender when it comes to emotions and connection, I was able to throw myself into my friendships without too much thought. However, as I got older, and puberty and adolescence hit, I became more aware of what was expected of me as a young man – from my family and my society. That was when I became self-conscious about being perceived as weak or girly. I often look back on those times now and wonder how on earth I came to such conclusions!

This self-consciousness lasted beyond my childhood in Nigeria and right into my early adulthood as a student at university in the UK. I attended a university reunion recently and it was amazing and gut-wrenching at the same time. We were all excited about seeing each other again after more than fourteen years but, of course, it brought back memories from my time studying. It made me think of the friendships I had then and how some of them were positive, but the majority were rather toxic. I tried so hard to fit in by creating a version of myself that even I could not recognise. There was this one guy I really wanted to be friends with, and this was purely because he was deemed 'popular' – he was the guy everyone wanted to be around. He saw right through my desperation and most certainly used it to his advantage. I found myself becoming a dogsbody to him, and (though this didn't matter to me then, since I was getting the recognition I felt I required) it led to a pretty tough time at university overall. When I look back now, I can, hand on heart, say I did not enjoy a single bit of it, even though I tricked myself into believing it was the best time of my life.

I would turn up at the student union bar to spend all the money I didn't have. (I'm talking about overdrafts from my various student accounts. Back then banks used to throw student accounts at freshers.) I spent all that money because I wanted to fit in, I wanted to be accepted. Spending like that meant I came out of university with huge debts, debts I ran away from, which of course led to defaults and negative marks on my credit file. We all know how this can impact you later in life and I did not get on top of it all until my early thirties.

In an article published on the website for Equinox (a residential treatment centre for adolescent boys struggling with trauma and addictive behaviours) I read about male friendship in a way that really resonated with me: 'When male friendships are discussed, they are often relegated to the superficial category of buddies and described as a network of peers where sharing and emotional support isn't part of the narrative. These friendships are often depicted as pals interested in playing sports, competing against one another, and discussing various conquests in life, rather than as deep emotional bonds that thrive on sharing their inner lives. These depictions are defined by their simplicity and do not account for any emotional nuance or depth. However, when researchers actually talked to adolescent boys, they found that males do desire developing friendships where secrets are shared, that friendships are essential for their mental health, and the loss of these friendships through adolescence is painful for them.'[27]

The article goes on to explain the concept of 'shoulder-to-shoulder' friendships – which are generally experienced by men – versus 'face-to-face' friendships, which tend to be experienced by women. Of course, this is a broad generalisation, and friendship certainly shouldn't be gendered so obviously, but it is what it is. This is how many of us have been socialised.

'Should-to-shoulder' relationships can be described as friendships built around shared interests, such as gaming or sports. Picture it: a few men sitting side-by-side, enjoying a match together. Conversation tends to be limited to topics related to whatever activity the friends are enjoying together, and it's rare that things get any deeper than that. For me, personally, I would say that my relationships in university were more like this, built around the shared interests of partying and women.

On the other hand, 'face-to-face' friendships revolve more around conversation, vulnerability, and disclosing personal information, thoughts, and feelings. These kinds of friendships are more open and vulnerable. No concept of friendship is perfect, but experts have found that when men are able to engage on a more emotional level with their friends like this, the benefits impact physical and mental health.

Over the years, as I have grown older and wiser, I have found myself actively seeking out meaningful male connections – connections where we are not shoulder-to-shoulder but face-to-face. Connections that provide those in my friendship groups the opportunity to be vulnerable without fear of any kind of reproach. These friendship groups provide a safe space for us all to just be, to not act or try to fit in, and, most importantly, it provides a space where we can all give advice and be truthful to each other. What I have found is, this also promotes accountability and a lack of ego.

To get here, I had to be intentional about my choice of friends. I had to be intentional about pretty much everything. I read, in a book titled *Atomic Habits* by James Clear, that, 'Every choice you make becomes a habit that then is a vote for the future self you want to be.'[28]

I laugh every time a friend of Candice asks me to hook her up with a male friend of mine. I respond by saying I do not have friends who are single! This is not to say that your lack of a significant other automatically disqualifies you from being my friend, I am just saying

HONEST AND OPEN RELATIONSHIPS ARE KEY TO HAVING ACCOUNTABILITY IN YOUR LIFE – AND ACCOUNTABILITY WILL KEEP YOU ON TRACK.

I have gone out of my way to surround myself with like-minded people, and this is why we can all be honest and open with each other.

Honest and open relationships are key to having accountability in your life – and accountability will keep you on track. One of my friends, who holds me the most accountable, is a woman, Tolani. She's my best friend and we have been friends for years. I remember, shortly after Esmé was born, Candice and I had an argument. I stormed out of my house and went to Tolani and my other friend, Ladi. Now, Ladi was commiserating with me, as men tend to do with each other. 'You know how women can be…' etc. But Tolani challenged me. 'What did you do?' she asked. 'What was your contribution?'

It's a question she has asked me since university days. Whenever I got into an altercation or argument, her response was always, 'What part did you play in that?' You might wonder why I'd stay such good friends with someone who never seems to be 'on my side', but the way she challenges me and holds me accountable makes me a better version of myself and is ultimately in my best interests. She never allows me to take the easy way out and, thanks to her, this idea of accountability and owning my shit is now a way of life for me. Something can happen and, while I'm not entirely to blame, I still need to ask myself, *what part did I play?*

And it's important to answer this question from the other person's perspective. From where they stand, what harm have I caused and how did I make them feel? So much of life is about perspective and one's ability or inability to actually see something from another person's perspective. Things become a whole lot easier when you're able to have that wider view of the situation. And this is how I was able to reconcile with Candice after that blow-up, and how I've been able to reconcile the most important relationships in my life.

After being an idiot in my relationship with Renae's mum, trying to see things from her perspective is pretty much the only thing that has helped to fix our relationship in the years since we split up. There was a lot of friction initially, as is common for many of us trying to co-parent. But it was when I decided to view the breakdown of our relationship from her perspective that we were able to move beyond that. I had to go to her and be like, 'Listen, looking at it from your perspective, I did fuck up. Please forgive me, I'm not that person anymore.' Whether she would choose to believe that was not my business at the time. I just had to stop blaming her and hold myself accountable for the ways that I caused hurt and for how I made her feel. That conversation changed our relationship to what it is now. We are genuinely good friends and, while, of course, Renae's wellbeing is our primary concern, we can talk about anything outside of that as two friends.

Besides the friendships that we choose, our families obviously play a massive part in our lives. Most of my birth family are in a completely different country to me. Thanks to the wonders of technology, I speak to my dad three or four times a week, and my mum near enough on a daily basis via video call. Whenever anyone can visit us in the UK, they do, and while there was definitely a time where this didn't feel enough and I missed my birth family a lot, that feeling of not having

THE IDEA OF FAMILY IS WHAT YOU MAKE IT

enough people around me has disappeared over the years. I've created my own family, my own village, separate from my birth family, and I truly believe that the idea of family is what you make it.

You've probably heard the phrase, 'blood is thicker than water', which suggests that our family relationships are the most important in our lives, but modern commentators believe that the original phrase is, 'the blood of the covenant is thicker than the water of the womb'. They say this actually means that the bonds created by mutual agreement (originally meant during warfare, i.e. between soldiers serving together) are actually stronger than traditional family ties. I wholeheartedly believe this. Yes, our families are important, and if you have a great relationship with them, all the better! But the spine of my community is the people I have chosen to journey through life with. The ones I know I can depend on and who share the same path as me.

Some of these people are miles ahead of me, and I can learn from them. Some of them are walking side-by-side with me. And maybe some have not reached where I am just yet. But the fact that we are all facing the same way, so to speak, aiming for the same things, makes their presence in my life invaluable. And this isn't just a material or financial thing. We might actually be in different places on paper, but our morals, ethics, and outlooks align, and we can encourage each other and empathise with each other along the way. As I mentioned before, I've chosen to surround myself with (mostly) men who are married or in long-term relationships, with young families, and who are striving to be better versions of themselves (or their fathers). We all think or function in a certain way that is conducive to the lives we are trying to build, and this community has come about by me being intentional and choosing to be around them. But of course, we're not cookie-cutter copies of each other. There is variety in terms of background, race, and gender, and that brings another level of richness to my chosen family and community.

Another habit of mine, that I have mentioned time and again in this book, is therapy! I never used to be that open to the idea of therapy, or psychotherapy to be exact, but it has become an integral part of my self-care routine, and it is now a recurring monthly bill of mine.

I remember the day I told Mum I had started therapy. Her response was not surprising at all – I expected it. Her words were, 'God forbid! There is nothing wrong with you. You do not need therapy – in Jesus's name!' I laughed so hard once she was done. I even told her that I recommended it to her as well and she threatened to give me a knock on my head the next time she saw me.

I know where Mum's reaction comes from. The traditional attitude toward therapy makes it a taboo subject, something to be ashamed of, even though it is something most people simply do not understand. The general consensus seems to be: you can either pray away any issue you may have or ignore it by being a strong person. If you decide to partake in any form of therapy, then there must be something wrong with you. And if, for any reason, people find out, you and your parents then become the talk of the town. I do find this rather annoying though, because I believe this sort of thinking is tied to religion.

When I was younger and a churchgoer back home, I distinctly remember pastors praying away the 'evil spirits of depression', and various vigils and prayer sessions for individuals who dared to mention the fact that they were dealing with depression. But for me, finding therapy has been my lightbulb moment. Therapy has helped me understand who I really am. It has helped me deal with past trauma that I somehow hid and didn't realise was manifesting in another way. Most importantly, it has helped me understand that, as a human being, I am not without complexity and so is everyone else, most especially Dad. And lastly, therapy has helped me understand that it is simply not enough to just want to do the opposite of what Dad did, but to lean into and draw from the qualities he displayed that I admire while understanding that the qualities I deem as unacceptable can be ignored. After all, I cannot expect five gallons of water from a one-gallon bottle.

I say all of the above to say this: I have never been more sure of who I am and what my purpose is than I am now. And all of this is because of the active steps I have taken to understand what makes me who I am. If there is a word to define how I have decided to live over the last few years it is 'intentionally'. This was made possible by therapy, spirituality, friends, and friendship groups. All these factors together helped in my battle of fault versus responsibility: it is not my fault or Dad's that he raised me the way he did, but it is damn sure my responsibility to ensure that I do what I feel is right with my children, that I do what I feel is right to be a better husband and partner, to be a better friend, and to be a better person. Because if I don't, all I will be doing is carrying on that wave of transgenerational trauma.

Listen, therapy is so important! We all need it. And now – speaking specifically to the Black community – we really, really need it! We're all traumatised in one way or another and we need to work through it. I wish people were more open to that, especially the older folks in our community. Therapists are trained professionals who have a balanced view and aren't there to take sides – what safer space is there than that?

Maybe this is a strange note on which to end a book on fatherhood, but I think it's important to be honest and real with you. In my quest to be the best version of a father I can be, avoiding the mistakes my father made and rebuilding the script for masculinity and fatherhood in my mind, I lost myself in the idea of fatherhood. Generally speaking, I have a one-track mind. I didn't have the ability to focus on more than one thing at the same time in the past. But therapy has helped me understand that it's okay to marry both versions of myself – the old pre-fatherhood me, and the new me, father to three beautiful kids. Part of doing this meant picking up hobbies and interests that allowed me to unplug, unwind, and separate myself from fatherhood in the moment. That is self-care and tending to myself, and it is vital. I can't pour out into my kids if my own cup is empty.

I am a limb of my family and my community, a vital part with an important function. If you have one part of any system, whether it's a body or a computer, and it's malfunctioning, eventually the entire system will feel it and be stunted in its function – if it doesn't break down altogether! I need to be the best version of myself, to give the best of myself, to make this whole thing work.

My dad wasn't the best version of himself while I was growing up. He had trauma he hadn't dealt with, and he was embodying the traditional ideas of masculinity that he thought were necessary. He felt like he was doing the best that he could, but it wasn't enough for me. I can honestly say that, with maturity, space for self-reflection, and professional support in addressing past traumas, I am finally correcting the path that I was so scared of following.

FATHERHOOD IN ACTION

I can safely say that my idea of being a great parent requires the creation of an amazing support system. Who do you rely on to support you as you work on being the best parent you can be? Here are a few questions to ask yourself about the people you surround yourself with. They will help you assess who your non-family family are.

- **Accountability.** Are you comfortable enough to hold each other accountable when necessary?

- **Competition.** Is there constant competition or rivalry within your network or group of friends?

- **Vulnerability.** Can you be vulnerable around them and not worry about feeling judged?

- **Dependability.** Are they dependable?

- **Loyalty.** Are they loyal to you?

- **Trust.** Do you trust them?

ENDNOTES

1   (p25) King's College Lagos. Accessed March 2020. https://kingscollegelagos.com.ng/about-us.

2   (p48) Carson, Gordon. "Effect of early trauma on parenting skills". *Community Care*. September 2011. https://www.communitycare.co.uk/2011/09/15/effect-of-early-trauma-on-parenting-skills.

3   (p55) hooks, bell. *All About Love: New Visions*. William Morrow, 2000.

4   (p72) Weitz, Paul and Stevens, Dana. *Fatherhood*. Columbia Pictures, June 2021.

5   (pp78–79) Powledge, Tabitha M. "Behavioral Epigenetics: How Nurture Shapes Nature". *BioScience*, vol. 61, no. 8. August 2011. https://doi.org/10.1525/bio.2011.61.8.4.

6   (p83) Fathering in 15. "Fathering Skills". *National Fatherhood Initiative*. Accessed March 2022. https://cdn2.hubspot.net/hubfs/135704/Miscellaneous%20Documents/F15/09%20Fathering%20Skills.pdf.

7   (p85) Morin, Amy. "What is Toxic Masculinity?", *Verywell Mind*. November 2020. https://www.verywellmind.com/what-is-toxic-masculinity-5075107.

8   (pp85–86) Franco, Fabiana. "Understanding Intergenerational Trauma: An Introduction for Clinicians". *Good Therapy*. January 2021. https://www.goodtherapy.org/blog/Understanding_Intergenerational_Trauma.

9   (p99) Friedman, Uri. "How Much Do Parents Matter?" *The Atlantic*. September 2016. https://www.theatlantic.com/family/archive/2016/09/do-parents-matter-world/499808/.

10 (p112) Moynihan, Daniel Patrick. *The Negro Family: The Case For National Action*. US Department of Labor, March 1965.

11 (p112) Swan, L. Alex. "A Methodological Critique of the Moynihan Report". *The Black Scholar*, vol. 5, no. 9. June 1974. http://www.jstor.org/stable/41065735.

12 (pp112–114) Obama, Barack. Father's Day Speech, 2008. Chicago. Accessed on *Politico*, March 2022. https://www.politico.com/story/2008/06/text-of-obamas-fatherhood-speech-011094.

13 (p114) Levs, Josh. "No, Most Black Kids are Not Fatherless". *Huffington Post*. July 2016. https://www.huffpost.com/entry/no-most-black-kids-are-no_b_11109876.

14 (pp114–115) Jones, Jo and Mosher, William D. "Fathers' Involvement with their Children: United States, 2006–2010". *National Health Statistics Reports*, no. 71. National Center for Health Statistics. December 2013. https://www.cdc.gov/nchs/data/nhsr/nhsr071.pdf.

15 (p118) Knight, Marian et al. "Saving Lives, Improving Mothers' Care". MBRRACE-UK. Maternal, Newborn and Infant Clinical Outcome Review Programme. *National Perinatal Epidemiology Unit, University of Oxford*. November 2021. https://www.npeu.ox.ac.uk/assets/downloads/mbrrace-uk/reports/maternal-report-2021/MBRRACE-UK_Maternal_Report_2021_-_FINAL_-_WEB_VERSION.pdf.

16 (p127) University of Minnesota. "Involving Children in Household Tasks: Is it Worth the Effort?", *University of Minnesota*, September 2002. https://ghk.h-cdn.co/assets/cm/15/12/55071e0298a05_-_Involving-children-in-household-tasks-U-of-M.pdf.

17 (pp132, 140–142) Patton, Stacey. "Corporal punishment in black communities: Not an intrinsic cultural tradition but racial trauma". *American Psychological Association*. April 2017. https://www.apa.org/pi/families/resources/newsletter/2017/04/racial-trauma.

18 (p135) Glicksman, Eve. "Physical Discipline is Harmful and Ineffective". *American Psychological Association*. May 2019. https://www.apa.org/monitor/2019/05/physical-discipline.

19 (p141) Busari, Dauda Adaremi et al. "Cultural concepts employed in child discipline within rural Yorùbá households: the Ayetoro-Oke African community". *Rural Society*, vol. 26, no. 2. May 2017. https://doi.org/10.1080/10371656.2017.1340142.

20 (p142) Steele, Lauren. "How Child Discipline has Changed: A Brief History". *Fatherly*. Januar2018. https://www.fatherly.com/parenting/how-child-discipline-has-changed-a-brief-history.

21 (p142) Hill, Evan et al. "How George Floyd Was Killed in Police Custody". *New York Times*. May 2020 https://www.nytimes.com/2020/05/31/us/george-floyd-investigation.html.

22 (p143) Heilmann A. et al. "Physical Punishment and Child Outcomes: A Narrative Review of Prospective Studies". *The Lancet*, vol. 398, no. 10297. July 2021. https://doi.org/10.1016/S0140-6736(21)00582-1.

23 (p143) Ansell, Ali. "Physical Punishment Does Not Improve Behavior, Study Finds". *Very Well Family*. July 2021. https://www.verywellfamily.com/physical-punishment-does-not-improve-behavior-study-finds-5192520.

24 (p148) Hoecker, Jay L. Mayo Clinic Q&A. *Mayo Clinic*. Accessed March 2022. https://www.mayoclinic.org/healthy-lifestyle/infant-and-toddler-health/expert-answers/terrible-twos/faq-20058314.

25 (p157) United Nations. "Gender Equality". *UN Global Compact*. Accessed March 2022. https://www.unglobalcompact.org/what-is-gc/our-work/social/gender-equality.

26 (p171) Mental Health Foundation, "Work-life balance". *Mental Health Foundation*. Updated 21 September 2021. Accessed March 2022. https://www.mentalhealth.org.uk/a-to-z/w/work-life-balance.

27 (p198–199) Gillett, Kyle. "The Crisis of Connection: The Value of Male Friendships". *Equinox*. Accessed March 2022. https://equinoxrtc.com/blog/the-crisis-of-connection-the-value-of-male-friendships.

28 (p200) Clear, James. *Atomic Habits*. Random House Business, 2018.

FURTHER READING

Achebe, Chinua. *Things Fall Apart*. William Heinemann, 1958.

Akala. *Natives: Race and Class in the Ruins of Empire*. Two Roads, 2019.

Clear, James. *Atomic Habits*. Random House Business, 2018.

Coelho, Paulo. *The Alchemist*. HarperCollins, 1993.

Covey, Stephen R. *The Seven Habits of Highly Effective People*. Free Press, 1989.

Hardach, Sophie. "The Secret of Being a Good Father". BBC Future, June 2019.

Manson, Mark. *The Subtle Art of Not Giving a F*ck: A Counterintuitive Approach to Living a Good Life*. HarperOne, 2016.

Obama, Barack. *A Promised Land*. Viking, 2020.

Obama, Barack and Springsteen, Bruce. *Renegades: Born in the USA*. Viking, 2021. Accompanying podcast: "Renegades: Born in the USA", Higher Ground.

Obama, Michelle. "The Michelle Obama Podcast", Higher Ground.

Pinkett Smith, Jada et al. "Red Table Talk", Facebook Watch series.

Shetty, Jay. "On Purpose with Jay Shetty", podcast.

Smith, Will. *Will*. Century, 2021.

RESOURCES

BAATN (The Black, African and Asian Therapy Network)
www.baatn.org.uk

Black Mental Health Alliance
www.blackmentalhealth.com

Black Minds Matter
www.blackmindsmatteruk.com

Inclusive Therapists
www.inclusivetherapists.com

Latinx Therapy
www.latinxtherapy.com

Mind
www.mind.org.uk/information-support/drugs-and-treatments/
talking-therapy-and-counselling/how-to-find-a-therapist

National Child Traumatic Stress Network
www.nctsn.org

National Responsible Fatherhood Clearinghouse
www.fatherhood.gov

NHS (National Health Service, UK)
www.nhs.uk/service-search/mental-health/find-a-psychological-
therapies-service

Psychology Today: Find a Therapist
www.psychologytoday.com/us

SAMHSA (The Substance Abuse and Mental Health Services Administration)
www.samhsa.gov/find-help/national-helpline

Spare the Kids
www.sparethekids.com

Therapy for Black Men
www.therapyforblackmen.org

INDEX

ACKNOWLEDGMENTS

Something that has remained with me as I have grown from a boy to a man is the act of gratitude, so here goes...

I would first of all like to thank God for his protection and second chances.

Mum, my first love – it goes without saying that you are a visionary and I thank you for this.

My therapist – thank you for the work you put into getting me to reconcile all parts of myself. Without you, none of this would have been possible.

Cupcake – You – where do I even begin? I remain forever grateful for that day you agreed to give me your WhatsApp details – look at all we have created together.

Renae, Esmé-Olivia, and Richard-Junior – being Daddy to you guys is not only a privilege, it is also a blessing. I remain thankful for your guidance on how to be the best version of the kind of father that you require.

Oyebade and Oyeyode, my beloved sisters – thank you for your patience and understanding.

Dad – thank you Pops – we may not have seen eye to eye while I was growing up, but here we are, constantly learning.

Sam – thank you for giving me the chance to redeem myself and play an active role in the life of my daughter.

Mayode – Sule – I love you Bro, thank you for your prayers and words of encouragement.

The Brotherhood WhatsApp Group – guys, we are on a journey, and what a journey it has been thus far. Thank you for the accountability, the openness, and the truths we are all ready to share and receive – long may our brotherhood continue.

Tolani and Ladi – my pillars – I love you both.

Craig and Sean – I met you both during my professional journey and we have gone from colleagues to BFFs. Thank you for your advice and friendship over the years.

Jendella Benson – my sensei, I never saw myself as capable of writing or telling a story that is worthy enough. You held my hands every step the way and asked for more when you felt I was holding back. This is all possible because of you – for this I am eternally grateful.

Stephanie Milner – you knew I had a story to tell before I even realised and, despite my excuses and ducking and diving, you were relentless and absolutely right as well. Thank you for taking a chance on me.

Remi Sade – thank you for being a sounding board and a constant source of encouragement and strategy.

Leeanne Adu – thank you for ensuring that the work got done.

Francesca Zampi and Katie-Jane Sullivan – thank you both for being incredibly supportive agents and friends.

Steve Kingsley – last but certainly not least – I bloody did it! Thank you for giving me that much needed push.

ABOUT THE AUTHOR

Bodé Aboderin is a writer, influencer, speaker, businessman, investor, and stay-at-home dad.

Following his recent conversion from climbing the corporate ladder, Bodé is on a mission to communicate his rapidly changing beliefs on fatherhood and masculinity in real-time.

Originally from Nigeria, Bodé now lives in Milton Keynes with his wife, children, and pet dog. Alongside running a household and family business, managing the school schedules, feeding the family, and staying on top of a mountain of laundry, he also runs a growing media business with his wife, Candice Brathwaite, supporting and championing her plans for world domination.

Recently bestowed with the honour of being the only male speaker at Pregnant Then Screwed – a festival celebrating mothers with careers – Bodé is shifting the narrative on what it means to be a father in the present day.

SHIFTING THE NARRATIVE

Publishing Director Katie Cowan
Art Director Maxine Pedliham
Senior Acquisitions Editor Stephanie Milner
Design Manager Bess Daly
Project Editor Kiron Gill
Editor Jendella Benson
Copy Editor Shari Last
Proofreader and Indexer Elizabeth Dowsett
DTP Designers Satish Gaur, Anurag Trivedi, Pushpak Tyagi
Designer Amy Cox
Jacket Illustrator Sol Cotti
Jacket Design STUDIO ROY
Jackets Coordinator Jasmin Lennie
Pre-Production Manager Sunil Sharma
Senior Production Editor Tony Phipps
Senior Production Controller Samantha Cross

First American Edition, 2022
Published in the United States by DK Publishing
1745 Broadway, 20th Floor, New York, NY 10019

Copyright © 2022 Dorling Kindersley Limited
DK, a Division of Penguin Random House
22 23 24 25 26 10 9 8 7 6 5 4 3 2
001–326300–Jun/2022

Text copyright © 2022 Bodé Aboderin
Bodé Aboderin has asserted his right to be identified as the author of this work.

DK books are available at special discounts when purchased in bulk for sales
promotions, premiums, fund-raising, or educational use. For details, contact:
DK Publishing Special Markets, SpecialSales@dk.com.

A catalog record for this book is available
from the Library of Congress.
ISBN 978-0-7440-4814-8

Printed and bound in the United Kingdom

For the curious
www.dk.com

This book was made with Forest
Stewardship Council™ certified
paper – one small step in DK's
commitment to a sustainable future.
For more information go to
www.dk.com/our-green-pledge